C0-ATR-927

HOUSEHOLD
WASTE
RECYCLING

HOUSEHOLD
WASTE
RECYCLING

RICHARD WAITE

EARTHSCAN

Earthscan Publications Ltd, London

First published in 1995 by
Earthscan Publications Limited
120 Pentonville Road, London N1 9JN

Copyright © Richard Waite, 1995

All rights reserved. No part of this book may be reproduced in any form without written
permission from the publisher and author.

A catalogue record for this book is available from the British Library

ISBN: 1 85383 242 1

Typeset by DP Photosetting, Aylesbury, Bucks
Printed and bound in Great Britain by
Biddles Ltd, Guildford and King's Lynn.

Earthscan Publications Limited is an editorially independent subsidiary of Kogan Page
Limited, and publishes in association with the International Institute for Environment
and Development and the World Wide Fund for Nature.

363. 7282
W145h

CONTENTS

◆

LIST OF ILLUSTRATIONS

◆

Figures

Tables

GLOSSARY

◆

Terms

Air classification   An industrial technique for separating light materials from heavy materials by passing them over an air jet.

Anaerobic decomposition   The breakdown of organic material in the absence of oxygen.

Anaerobic digestion   The controlled process of anaerobic decomposition.

Avoided collection and disposal savings   The costs of refuse collection and disposal which are not incurred by a WCA or WDA respectively as a result of waste being diverted for recycling or recovery.

Bank   A collection container used in a drop-off scheme.

Blue Box   A system of kerbside collection of dry recyclables, typically using one or two 50 litre collection containers.

Bring scheme   A system in which householders bring source separated recyclable materials to designated collection points, also called a drop-off scheme.

Calorific value   The energy content of a material or mixture of materials, measured in megajoules per kilogramme (MJ/kg).

Civic Amenity Site   A site provided by a WDA in accordance with s51 of the EPA or by a WCA at which the public may deposit waste.

Closed loop recycling   The use of recycled material to produce a product which is identical to the product which was previously recycled.

Commercial waste	Waste defined in s75 of the EPA as arising from premises which are not private households or industrial premises, for example shops and restaurants.
Commingled collection	The collection of a mixture of waste materials.
Composite packaging	Packaging produced from one or more materials which are not readily separable.
Composting	The natural decomposition of organic material in the presence of oxygen.
Controlled waste	Household, commercial and industrial waste as defined in s75 of the EPA.
Cullet	Processed glass.
De-inking	The removal of ink from waste paper following pulping.
Digestate	Organic material residue resulting from the process of anaerobic digestion.
District heating scheme	A system in which a large number of properties are linked to a single large scale source of heating.
Diversion rate	The amount of material diverted from disposal by recycling or recovery, measured as a percentage of total waste arisings.
Drop-off scheme	A system in which householders bring source separated recyclable materials to designated collection points, also called a bring scheme.
Dry recyclables	Recyclable materials comprising paper and board, plastics, metals, glass and textiles.
Dustbin waste	Household waste collected free of charge by a WCA from every household under the regular (normally weekly) refuse collection service.
Eco-tax	A tax on products which do not meet defined environmental criteria. First introduced in Belgium.
Eddy current separation	An electrical technique for separating aluminium by inducing an electrical eddy current in the aluminium which is then repulsed electromagnetically, literally ejecting the aluminium.
Fraction	A designated proportion of the wastestream.
Global warming	The raising of the temperature of the earth's atmosphere as a result of the action of greenhouse gases.
Green Bag	A system of kerbside collection of dry recyclables using plastic bags or sacks as the collection containers.
Green Bin	A system of kerbside collection of dry recyclables and/or organics typically using one or more standard or divided 240 litre wheeled bins.
Greenhouse gas	A gas which has the potential to act to increase the temperature of the earth's atmosphere.
Head-on sorting	A processing technique in which a mixture of three different materials are presented to a sorting operator

on a conveyor which brings the material towards rather than past the operator.

High density bring scheme A drop-off scheme with a high density of collection points, density being measured in terms of the number of sites or containers per head of population.

Hydrocyclone An industrial device for separating materials on the basis of their relative densities.

Integrated collection The separate collection of both recyclable materials and refuse in a single RCV.

Intensive banking A drop-off scheme with a high density of collection points, density being measured in terms of the number of sites or containers per head of population.

Kerbside scheme The collection of a range of recyclable materials from individual households following source separation of these materials.

Landfill cover A layer of inert material deposited each day to cover waste which has been landfilled.

Landfill gas A mixture of methane and carbon dioxide generated within landfill sites as a result of anaerobic decomposition (also called biogas).

Landfill levy A surcharge on the cost of landfill measured in £/tonne.

Landfill site A site at which waste is deposited for permanent disposal.

Leachate Liquid generated within a landfill and which requires containment or treatment.

Material reprocessing The industrial treatment of recyclable materials in which the form of the material is changed in order to produce recycled materials.

Micro recycling centre A designated collection point in an intensive banking scheme.

Mini recycling centre A designated collection point in a drop-off scheme which allows the deposit of only a limited number of materials and which utilises collection containers which are smaller than those at a recycling centre but larger than those at a micro recycling centre.

Mixed refuse Refuse which has not been separated at source and which typically arises in the traditional dustbin.

Negative sorting Removing minority unwanted materials from commingled recyclable materials during processing, leaving the majority of the material to pass through the processing operation.

Organic material Kitchen or garden waste of an organic nature which is suitable for composting or anaerobic digestion.

Participation rate The percentage of householders who take part in a recycling scheme.

Picking station	A work place in a processing plant at which material is manually sorted.
Post-consumer waste	Waste which is generated because the product has reached the end of its useful life, that is products which have been used and discarded.
Processing	The treatment of collected recyclable materials prior to reprocessing.
Putrescibles	Organic material.
Reuse	Using a product more than once without changing its physical form.
Recyclable materials	Materials which have the potential to be recycled.
Recycled materials	Materials which have been recycled either by incorporation into a product or in the form of a secondary raw material.
Recycling centre	A designated collection point in a drop-off scheme.
Recycling credits	A financial credit payable by a WDA to a WCA or by a WCA to a WDA or by either to a third party in accordance with s52 of the EPA.
Recycling rate	The tonnage of waste recycled expressed as a percentage of total waste arisings.
Secondary raw material	Recycled material in the form of a raw material which is suitable for use in new product manufacture.
Source separation	The separation of recyclable materials into different fractions by the householder prior to collection.
Stickies	Adhesive materials which arise in waste paper pulping.
Sustainability	The use and consumption of the Earth's resources in a way which does not disadvantage future generations.
Transfer station	A facility to which loose refuse is delivered by RCVs and at which the refuse is transferred to larger bulk vehicles or containers for onward transport, normally for disposal.
Trippage rate	The number of times a product is reused.
Trommel screen	An industrial device for separating materials based on their physical size.
Virgin material	Raw material produced from previously unused sources, that is not recycled.
Waste analysis	The analysis of a sample of waste to determine its composition and the weight of the component fractions.
Waste arisings	The quantity of waste generated, usually measured in tonnes per annum.
Waste minimisation	Techniques to prevent waste being generated, also termed waste prevention (see also waste reduction).

Waste recycling plan	A plan produced by a WCA in accordance with s49 of the EPA, detailing how recycling is to be undertaken.
Waste reduction	Any technique which reduces the amount of waste (once generated) which has to be disposed of. Thus re-use and recycling are waste reduction techniques. Not to be confused with waste mimimisation.
Wheeled bin	A lidded refuse container fitted with wheels. If supplied to households by a WCA the householder is usually required to wheel the bin to the kerbside for collection.
Windrow	An elongated pile of organic material undergoing composting.

Acronyms and abbreviations

ACORN	A Classification Of Residential Neighbourhood Groups
ACRA	Aluminium Can Recycling Association
AD	anaerobic digestion
CAWDP	Civic Amenity Waste Disposal Project
CCT	compulsory competitive tendering
CHP	combined heat and power
COPAC	The Consortium of the Packaging Chain
DLO	Direct Labour Organisation
DoE	Department of the Environment
DSD	Duales System Deutschland
DSO	Direct Service Organisation
EPA	Environmental Protection Act
ERRA	European Recycling and Recovery Association
HDPE	high density polyethylene
HMIP	Her Majesty's Inspectorate of Pollution
KLS	Kraft lined strawboard (corrugated cardboard)
LAWDC	Local Authority Waste Disposal Company
LCA	life cycle analysis
LDPE	low density polyethylene
MRF	materials recovery facility
NFFO	non-fossil fuel obligation
PE	polyethylene
PET	polytetraphthalate
PRG	Producer Responsibility Industry Group
PS	polystyrene
PVC	polyvinyl chloride
RCV	refuse collection vehicle
RDF	refuse derived fuel
REL	rear-end loader

SELCHP	South East London Combined Heat and Power
SVM	Stichting Verpakking en Milieu
UBC	used beverage can
VALPAK	provisional name for UK packaging recovery organisation
WCA	waste collection authority
WDA	waste disposal authority
WRA	waste regulation authority
WTE	waste to energy

ACKNOWLEDGEMENTS

◆

I would like to thank Coopers & Lybrand for their assistance in the production of this book and for the encouragement and support that I have received during its preparation.

Anita Forster has performed miracles in converting my initial drafts into readable text and has also prepared many of the illustrations. My thanks to her.

I am grateful to a number of individuals, local authorities and private companies who have very kindly provided photographs to illustrate the book and I have acknowledged these in the text.

Finally, without the support and understanding of my wife Jennifer I would not have embarked upon my career in recycling and this book would not have been written. As ever, I am in her debt.

CHAPTER ONE

INTRODUCTION

—————————— ◆ ——————————

What is household waste?

This book is about household waste, the rubbish that you and I generate as individuals in our homes and which our local council is obliged to collect and dispose of on our behalf. We all know that we generate waste and when we stop to think about it, we feel that something could and ought to be done to reduce or recycle what we discard. However, very few of us actually know what happens to our waste now, let alone what could be done to reduce its environmental impact.

Household waste comprises those unwanted items which arise in a domestic dwelling: discarded products such as furniture, clothing or toys, used packaging, food leftovers, garden waste, the by-products of DIY and so on. Our local district or borough council is obliged to collect this material from our houses in whatever manner they deem appropriate and having collected it, to deliver it for disposal.

It is difficult to be precise about the amount of waste that we generate as even official published figures are based on estimates. This is illustrated in Table 1.1 which presents four recent analyses of UK waste arisings. If we take a figure for household waste of 20m tonnes per annum, this represents less than 5 per cent of the national total waste arisings. However, if the wastes from agriculture, mining and quarrying and ash, slag and sewage sludge are regarded as being disposed of within the respective industries, household waste may then be seen as a significant part (approximately 30–35 per cent) of the remaining industrial, commercial and household wastes (collectively known as controlled waste) which have to be disposed of. On average we generate one tonne of such waste per household every year.

Table 1.1 Annual UK waste arisings (million tonnes)

Sector	MSI Data 1991[1]	Gibb/ DoE 1989[2]	DoE 1992[3]	COPAC Action Plan[4]
Agriculture	262	250	80[3]	250
Mining and quarrying	137	130	108[4]	75[5]
Industrial	44	50	50	62[6]
Household	28	28[2]	20	26[7]
Commercial	19[1]		15	
Power station ash	16	14	13	12
Blast furnace slag	6	6	6	
Toxic	6			5
Sewage sludge		24	36	
Construction and demolition			32	
Building rubble		3		
Dredged spoils			43	
TOTAL	518	516	402	430

1 includes building waste; 2 includes trade waste; 3 refers to housed livestock only; 4 excludes waste from opencast coal mining; 5 mineral and coal extraction only; 6 includes commercial waste; 7 includes 7m tonnes of commercial waste

Despite the fact that household waste represents such a small proportion of our total waste arisings, it attracts a great deal of attention and concern, primarily because it is highly visible and because none of us can ignore its presence or our responsibility for its generation.

Household waste is collected using dustbins, plastic sacks or wheeled bins, depending on local arrangements. After collection, approximately 85 per cent is disposed of by burying it in landfill sites, 10 per cent is burned in incineration plants and less than 5 per cent is recycled. This latter method of treatment, that of recycling, while currently in the minority, is gaining in popularity. In the 1990 White Paper 'This Common Inheritance'[5] the government set a target of recycling 25 per cent of all household waste by the year 2000. This target is based on the premise that approximately one half of household waste is potentially recyclable, so that the target is in fact to recycle one half of this potentially recyclable fraction. Furthermore, Section 49 of the 1990 Environmental Protection Act requires every waste collection authority (district or borough council) to prepare a waste recycling plan. In England, these plans had to be submitted to the Department of the Environment for consideration by August 1992. While no date was set for Scottish or Welsh authorities, the majority of councils have prepared their plans. The legislative requirement for local authorities to prepare recycling plans has not yet been enacted in Northern Ireland.

Many local authorities have, in fact, taken the government's target as their own, even though there is no legal requirement for them to do so. However, having accepted the challenge, the majority of recycling plans demonstrate that under present circumstances the achievement of the target is unlikely.

Why recycling is important

The European Community (EC) Strategy for Waste Management (SEC (89) 934) which was adopted in May 1990, established a hierarchy of preferred waste management approaches which has now been universally adopted. In descending order of preference this hierarchy is:

1) waste minimisation;
2) material reuse;
3) material recycling;
4) energy recovery from waste; and
5) safe disposal.

The priority, quite rightly, is to reduce the amount of waste that we produce by minimising the quantities of natural resources that we convert into products and then discard. However, such an objective is diametrically opposed to the culture of our society. All western societies are consumer societies; we are encouraged, primarily by intensive advertising, to consume as many products as we can afford. The belief that this has engendered in us all is that new is best and old should be discarded. New products are continually being brought out and promoted as having an enhanced performance, reduced running costs or improved design or as incorporating the latest technological developments. This is true from washing powders to cameras and cars. Rarely, if ever, is a product designed to use fewer natural resources or for greater longevity. Our culture is one of consumption and of planned product obsolescence. The concept of waste minimisation is not, therefore, one which sits easily with our existing social habits.

Some progress is being made, for example in the area of packaging. The majority of packaging is designed to be disposed of once the product that it is protecting has reached its final destination, the consumer. The concept of waste minimisation when applied to this situation simply means designing the packaging so that it uses the minimum of resources to fulfil its function, so that when discarded, the minimum of waste is generated. This is gradually starting to happen and a number of examples are shown in Table 1.2.

Table 1.2 Examples of packaging light weighting

Packaging item	Unit weight (g) 1950s	1960s	1970s	1980s	1990s
Glass milk bottle	538	397	340	245	245
Glass jam jar	180	180	180	180	160
Steel food can	69	69	69	58	57
Metal drinks can	91	91	91	20	17
Plastic yoghurt pot			9	7	5
PET drinks bottle				66	42

Source: Biffa[6]

With regard to household waste, however, waste minimisation is very difficult to achieve. You and I as waste generators are not encouraged to reduce our waste, if anything the reverse is true. In addition, there is no penalty if we produce more waste, since whatever waste we set out for collection is taken away, and we all pay roughly the same for the collection and disposal service through our council tax (the only difference being as a result of council tax banding). This is a real problem for local authorities who are seeking to encourage householders to reduce the amount of waste they produce. Since householders do not pay for waste collection and disposal in proportion to the amount of waste they produce, there is no financial incentive to change their habits. Indeed even if such charges *were* linked to the quantity of waste generated, the average annual charge per household would only be of the order of £50–60.[7] How much effort will people make to save one pound per week? Apart from the fact that such a level of direct charge for waste collection and disposal is unlikely to significantly change householders' behaviour, there is also a very valid concern that less scrupulous householders might seek to avoid paying such charges by illegally disposing of their waste, for example through fly-tipping. The introduction of direct collection and disposal charges is thus unlikely in the foreseeable future, but should not be ruled out. The technology required to implement direct charging is available and trials in Europe and the USA have shown that fly-tipping can be contained. We should not therefore necessarily dismiss this approach to encouraging waste minimisation.

If we are to encourage greater waste minimisation amongst householders it will have to be supported by providing information and education. Indeed, it is true that the more people learn about recycling and begin to change their behaviour accordingly, the more aware they become of the need and opportunities for waste minimisation.

Having sought to minimise the amount of waste being generated, we must however accept that some waste will be generated and consider how best to treat such waste so as to limit its environmental impact. Any technique which reduces the amount of waste (once generated) which requires disposal is termed waste reduction – not to be confused with waste minimisation. This brings us to the second preference in the waste management hierarchy, that of material reuse.

Material reuse is an attractive approach, but does have severe limitations. The best known examples are those of milk bottles and beer bottles, where the system of delivering full bottles is also used to collect and return the empty bottles after use. Clearly, the opportunities for introducing similar system for other products or packaging formats are severely limited and even the two examples above are today in decline.

For a product reuse system to achieve an environmental performance that is superior to, for example, that of recycling, the number of times that the product is reused (the 'trippage rate') must be high. This is because of three environmental impacts that reusable containers have:

1) in order to survive multiple trips, the container must be thicker and stronger than the single trip equivalent, thereby consuming more raw material and energy in its original manufacture;

2) the transportation of heavier containers (including the return journey for refilling) uses more energy than the lighter, single trip equivalent; and

3) energy is needed to clean, sterilise and inspect the containers prior to refilling.

Provided that the trippage rate is high, these environmental impacts are less than those incurred by the use of single trip containers, even if such containers are recycled. The trippage rate for glass milk bottles in the UK is high, and is the prime example that we have of successful container reuse. The situation for glass beer bottles is however, very different. The average trippage rate for beer bottles has been falling in recent years, primarily because an increasing proportion of the market has been served by single trip bottles, many of which are foreign imports. At the same time there has been an increase in the provision of glass bottle banks, so that the collection of glass beer bottles for recycling has increased significantly. The combination of an increasing proportion of non-returnable glass bottles and a move towards collection for recycling rather than reuse, has resulted in the average trippage rate for returnable beer bottles falling as low as 4–5 trips. At such a low trippage rate, it is questionable whether the use of reusable glass bottles is environmentally preferable to single trip bottles which are recycled. When considering reuse systems it is thus always important to understand the trippage rate breakeven point, above which the superior environmental performance of reuse systems is achieved, and to ensure that such high trippage rates can be and are being achieved in practice.

An activity which has always been a part of our society, but which is today sadly also in decline and which is not often recognised as product reuse, is that of repairing products. Product repair prolongs the useful life of a product and can indeed provide a second or third life, as an alternative to disposal. The repair of consumer durables, for example furniture, electrical goods such as washing machines or audio equipment or mechanical products like clocks or lawnmowers was until relatively recently a large scale industry, employing many people at a local level. However, the move by industry in favour of designing products for ease of manufacture rather than repair (rendering many products virtually impossible to dis-assemble), together with the pressure on consumers to take advantage of a product's failure to replace it with a more up to date model, has seen the rapid decline of businesses offering repair services. Thus the opportunities for product reuse via a process of repair are today limited.

So we come to the third waste management option, that of material recycling, which is important for three reasons:

1) The recycling of waste to recover useful materials reduces our need for virgin raw materials. This has two benefits in that many raw material reserves are finite and the extraction or harvesting of such resources can in itself be extremely destructive to the environment. For example, the production of plastics from naturally occurring oil uses a finite resource (although the production of plastics accounts for only 4 per cent of oil usage, plastics packaging accounts for approximately one quarter of all plastics production). Aluminium is produced from bauxite, an abundant but finite resource and the mining of

which is extremely destructive to the environment where this ore occurs.

2) The reprocessing of waste materials can generate significant energy savings compared with the production of the equivalent virgin material. For example, producing new glass from cullet (broken, discarded glass) uses 25 per cent less energy (equivalent to 30 gallons of oil per tonne) than producing glass from the raw materials of silica sand, soda-ash and limestone. Equally, the production of new aluminium from aluminium scrap uses 95 per cent less energy than the smelting of bauxite ore.

3) Recycling reduces the amount of waste that requires disposal, thus reducing the environmental damage that waste disposal creates. Landfilling of waste can create ground water contamination via leakage of leachate (liquid arising from the waste) and air pollution through the generation of methane (a greenhouse gas) by the anaerobic degradation of organic material within the landfill. The incineration of waste gives rise to carbon dioxide and potentially toxic airborne emissions, as well as toxic solid waste in the form of ash. By recycling waste instead of disposing of it, we reduce these risks simply by reducing the amount of waste being disposed of. Less disposal means fewer disposals sites and where they already exist, their useful life can be prolonged.

Given the comments above on waste minimisation and material reuse, recycling can be seen as the best option we can hope for, for the majority of waste, given our society's continued preference for consumption. If we accept the view that we will continue to generate significant quantities of waste, then it is imperative that product designers take into consideration what will happen to a product at the end of its useful life and design features that facilitate the recycling of that product. For example, where a product, be it a child's toy, a portable radio, a car or simply the packaging of a product, is manufactured from more than one material, these materials must be easily and quickly identified and separated, if recycling is to be achieved. Such a design approach has not been taken in the past so that today, many recycling activities may be classed as 'end-of-pipe' solutions, that is, treating the symptoms not the cause. Only by designing for the 'life after death' of a product can many of the current barriers to the development of recycling be overcome.

The government's 25 per cent recycling target has encouraged recycling and has also generated much debate, part of which has focused on the definition of the word recycling. For many people the key question has been whether the definition of recycling includes energy recovery from waste, or whether it is limited to material recovery only. The government has clarified its position by stating that energy recovery is excluded as a means of achieving the 25 per cent target, but this position and the 25 per cent target itself are being reviewed as part of the development of a national waste management strategy.[8] Perhaps more importantly in a general sense, more precise definitions of what we mean by recycling have been developed and are becoming generally accepted.

The two key terms requiring definition are *recycling* and *recovery*. The definitions[9] published by the European Recycling and Recovery Association (ERRA) and which encapsulate the principles which are now generally accepted are as follows:

Recycling means to compost or regenerate materials for the original purpose or for other purposes, but excluding energy recovery.

Recovery means to recycle, compost, regenerate or to extract the energy to be used as an energy source (in accordance with Annex IIB [of the EC directive on Waste] 75/442/ECC).

As we will see in later chapters, the terminology of recycling is still evolving, so that the same word may mean different things to different people. However, standardisation is developing (much of this work being led by ERRA) and in this book the terms and definitions used reflect this growing standardisation.

Keeping recycling in context

The recycling of waste makes environmental sense, provided of course that the process of recycling does not itself create more environmental damage than that which is avoided by not disposing of the waste. But while we should seek to maximise environmentally beneficial recycling, there will always be a need for the disposal of some household waste which cannot be recycled, either because the waste materials are too contaminated to be reprocessed or because such recycling would incur an excessive financial or environmental cost.

Given that the need for waste disposal will continue, it is important to ensure that the environmental impacts of such activities are minimised. The two primary methods of waste disposal are *incineration* and *landfill*. If we return to the EC waste management hierarchy, the fourth preferred option is energy recovery from waste; that is, if we cannot recycle the material we should at least recover the energy content of the waste prior to disposal. Some of the incinerators built in the past and of the proposed new generation of waste incinerators are based on this principle. The waste is burned to produce heat which can either be used directly to provide heating to local buildings or indirectly to generate electricity. Either way, energy is recovered from the waste.

To a lesser extent, energy can also be recovered from waste which has been disposed of in a landfill site. When buried the organic elements of the waste decompose and since this happens in the absence of oxygen, methane gas is generated. Such gas generation is one of the problems of landfilling, but if the gas is collected it can be burned as a fuel, again recovering some energy from the waste.

Thus, if we cannot recycle some waste as material, we can at least seek to recover its energy content prior to its disposal.

Recycling should be seen, therefore, as the means by which we seek to minimise the environmental impact of both raw material production and waste disposal and should not be seen as a panacea for our waste disposal problems. Recycling must be kept in context; it is only one of the four elements of waste management of minimisation, reuse, recovery (material or energy) and disposal. Each element has a part to play and is inextricably linked to the other three. Indeed, while there has been an increasing level of promotion and support for recycling in the last few years, recently some people have begun to question the original EC waste hierarchy with regard to whether material recycling is in fact environmentally preferable to energy recovery. Evidence of such questioning came in the 26th report of the House of Lords Select Committee on the European Communities and which stated that

> in the light of the evidence we received we believe that this view of the hierarchy of waste management is simplistic and environmentally unsound: simplistic because it overlooks or does not attempt to quantify the benefits and disadvantages of particular courses of action; and environmentally unsound because it may lead to a greater consumption of resources than would result from the alternative disposals together with replacement by virgin materials.[10]

This view was echoed by the House of Commons Environment Select Committee in the report of their inquiry into recycling in 1993/94 in which the committee stated that

> The relative merits of energy and materials recovery, however, are finely balanced and will depend very much on the circumstances.[11]

One of the primary reasons for the increasing challenge to recycling as the preferred method of recovery is the growing acceptance that a significant proportion of household waste cannot in practical terms be recycled. Such practical limitations comprise:

- technical constraints such as contamination or commingling of materials;
- excessive financial costs, for example having to transport very lightweight materials over long distances to reach reprocessing facilities; and
- environmental impacts such as high energy usage, which would negate the environmental benefit of recycling such materials.

There is thus a growing realisation that there are technical, financial and environmental limitations to the extent to which household waste can and should be recycled. This is not to say that recycling is a bad thing or that energy recovery is the preferred method of treatment. It is clear that recycling has an important role to play in the management of our waste, but the extent of that role is limited and it is important that this is recognised and understood.

Sustainability

Sustainability is a concept about which much has been written and many words spoken but very little actually done. The need for action to achieve sustainability first came to prominence following the 1992 Rio Earth Summit, and in January 1994 the government published the UK strategy for sustainable development[12] which included a chapter on waste management. In simple terms, a sustainable approach is one which uses and consumes the Earth's resources in a way which does not disadvantage future generations.

Of late consideration has begun to be given to how this concept can be applied to waste management. For example the term 'sustainable landfill' has appeared.

The use of such terms however, suggests that the concept of sustainability is not being understood correctly. How can landfilling, which takes objects, many manufactured from finite resources, and entombs them in the ground under conditions which generate harmful gases and liquids for periods which are probably in excess of the life of the present generation, be considered as sustainable?

Sustainability is a key environmental goal for our society and is a goal which will be very hard to achieve. However, the mis-use of this term will devalue its importance and we must ensure that this does not happen. We have to develop sustainable methods of waste management, but at the same time accept that achieving this goal is a long way off, and in the interim we should implement techniques which have the minimal environmental impact.

About this book

In order to study the subject of recycling it is important first of all to understand the context in which recycling must operate. Chapter 2 describes how waste management activities are organised in the UK, identifies who is responsible for each activity and sets out some of the conflicts and barriers to the development of recycling that this has created.

By way of introduction to the specific subject of recycling, Chapters 3 and 4 address what can potentially be recycled from household waste and what the options are for dealing with such waste.

The three stages of recycling which convert recyclable materials into recycled materials are the collection of recyclable materials, the processing of collected materials and the reprocessing of individual materials. These stages are discussed individually in Chapters 5, 6 and 7 and the markets for recyclable materials are discussed in Chapter 8. The three elements of the recycling process are then brought together in Chapter 9 in order to analyse the key issue of what it costs to collect, process and reprocess household waste. The cost of recycling is one key measure of a recycling scheme: other such performance measures and proposals for standardising them to allow the comparison of schemes are discussed in Chapter 10.

Having discussed the recycling of all household waste, we then focus on one particular element which constitutes one of the largest components of household waste and which is currently receiving a great deal of attention, that of waste packaging. This material is highly visible and is the focus of much criticism. The future management of packaging waste is currently the subject both of EC legislation and of proposals for a national packaging recovery scheme, both of which could have major impacts not only on the packaging of goods, but also on the future approach to the recycling of all household waste. Chapter 11 therefore discusses this important and evolving issue.

In conclusion, the future development of household waste recycling in the UK is discussed in Chapter 12, in particular analysing the barriers to future development and presenting a summary of the actions needed for recycling to develop to the point where we can begin to achieve the levels of environmental benefit that many people are working to achieve and to which we all aspire.

CHAPTER TWO

HOW WASTE MANAGEMENT IS ORGANISED

——————————— ◆ ———————————

Waste management currently comprises three elements: recycling, waste collection and waste disposal. Before considering how recycling has developed and will develop and to provide a context for recycling, it is important for us to first consider how these other waste management activities are currently organised the UK.

Waste management is the responsibility of local authorities, such authorities being district or borough councils, county councils and metropolitan authorities. Waste collection is the responsibility of district or borough councils, in their capacity as waste collection authorities (WCAs) and waste disposal is the responsibility of county councils in their role as waste disposal authorities (WDAs). Metropolitan authorities, as unitary authorities, perform the roles of both WCA and WDA. The present two tier system of local government may change as a result of the Local Government Commission review, which could result in more local authorities becoming unitary authorities, so that the roles WCA and WDA will increasingly become the responsibility of a single authority.

Waste collection authorities

Each waste collection authority is responsible for organising the collection of household waste for its area and the delivery of this waste to a point of disposal as directed by the WDA. In the past, this work has been carried out by the local authority itself through its Direct Labour Organisation (DLO), however as a result of the Local Government Act of 1988, refuse collection services are now subject to compulsory competitive tendering (CCT). This requires that a contract for the provision of such services is put out to tender by the local authority on a regular basis, normally every five to seven years. This allows private sector firms to compete for the work of household waste collection, with the intention of ensuring that local authority-provided services are competitive.

In order to let a refuse collection contract, a local authority must draw up a clear and well defined contract specification which sets out exactly how the service is to be provided. The highly competitive nature of refuse collection contract tendering has resulted in the costs of collection being significantly reduced in many cases, but has also had the effect that any variation in the original contract specification will attract an additional cost. The implication of this for recycling is that if a local authority wishes to introduce changes to the agreed methods of refuse collection in order to introduce recycling, either the operational implications or the additional cost implications of such changes can prevent such changes being introduced within the life of an existing contract. This can have the effect of limiting the period when local authorities have an opportunity to introduce major changes for recycling. In other words, any proposed change in the methods of refuse collection in order to facilitate recycling are likely to be linked to the start of a new refuse collection contract and be incorporated within a revised collection contract specification.

With regard to recycling, the Environmental Protection Act (EPA) of 1990 introduced a new role for WCAs. Under Section 49 of the EPA, every WCA was given the duty to draw up a waste recycling plan. This requirement made it quite clear that the government had effectively given the responsibility for the recycling of household waste to WCAs. Many WCAs interpreted the requirement as the need to prepare a plan to show how the authority was going to achieve the government's target of recycling 25 per cent of household waste by the year 2000. Such an interpretation was in fact incorrect, both in terms of the plan content and because the target is a national, not a local one. The nature and content of the plans produced is discussed in detail later in this chapter.

Waste disposal authorities

The waste disposal authority role is fulfilled either by county councils or by groups of metropolitan authorities who come together in a joint board, or in the case of Scotland and Wales, the role is performed by individual unitary authorities. The WDA is responsible for both the provision of waste disposal facilities and the regulation of waste disposal activities, this second function being the responsibility of the authority in its capacity as a waste regulation authority (WRA). However in England, under the EPA, the roles of WDA and WRA have now been separated, as it was recognised that there is a potential conflict of interest when a single authority is responsible for both regulation and operation. As a result, metropolitan and county councils have either had to dispose of their waste disposal operations completely, or set up these operations as an arms' length company called a Local Authority Waste Disposal Company (LAWDC). A second requirement of the EPA is that all English WDAs must now subject their waste disposal operations to competitive tendering. If an authority chose to set up their in-house disposal operations as a LAWDC, this LAWDC is obliged to compete for the waste disposal contract in the same way as any other private sector organisation.

Since a LAWDC is a company wholly owned by a local authority, the finances of that company are directly linked to those of the parent authority. In particular, the ability of the LAWDC to raise capital through borrowing is constrained by the parent authority's borrowing limits. For this reason a number of authorities have sought to establish a joint venture arrangement between the LAWDC and a private sector waste management company, in order to make the LAWDC operations financially viable.

As with the collection of household refuse the above changes have had the effect of increasing the extent of private sector involvement in the disposal of household waste and there is an expectation that within a relatively short period of time, perhaps five years, the direct involvement of local authorities as providers of waste disposal facilities will have all but ceased. However, WDAs continue to be responsible for the provision of appropriate waste disposal facilities, through the letting of waste disposal contracts and having established such arrangements, are responsible for directing WCAs to the appropriate point of disposal.

This issue of WDA direction of WCAs raises an interesting point when the WCA wishes to direct their own collected household waste to an alternative location for the purposes of recycling. Under Section 48 (2) of the EPA, WCAs may direct waste to alternative locations for the purposes of recycling, unless the WDA has itself arranged for such waste to be recycled, in which case the WDA may invoke Section 48 (4) of the EPA and object to the WCA having such waste recycled.

Waste regulation authorities

In addition to its responsibility as a WDA, a county council or metropolitan authority also has responsibilities as a waste regulation authority. These responsibilities include site licensing, operations monitoring, regulation enforcement and waste planning. Of particular relevance to recycling is the waste disposal plan that the WRA is required to periodically produce and update under Section 50 of the EPA. The WRA has a duty to consult the WCAs on their recycling plans, and to take these plans into account when drawing up the waste disposal plan. It is the government's stated intention that the WRA responsibilities of local authorities will be transferred to the planned national Environmental Protection Agency, as and when this organisation is established.

The relationship between waste collection, waste disposal and waste regulation authorities is illustrated in Figure 2.1.

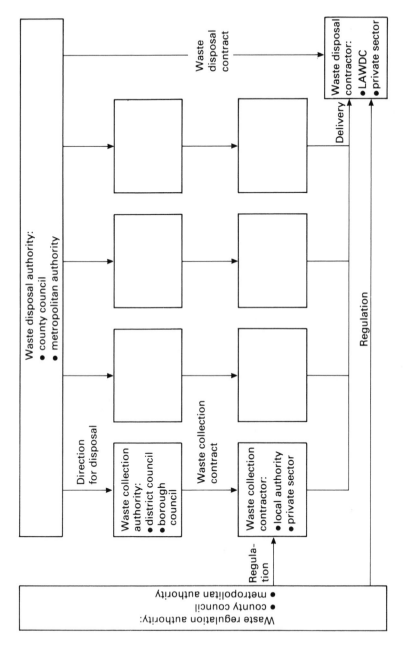

Figure 2.1 How waste management is organised

13

How waste management is paid for

The refuse collection contract entered into by a WCA is normally based on an annual fixed cost for the number of houses within that authority's geographical area. This cost, together with other district or borough council expenditure is then recovered from local residents through the council tax. This means that any household within a given council tax band will pay the same amount for refuse collection, irrespective of the amount of waste collected from that household.

The situation with waste disposal is somewhat more complex as each WDA provides waste disposal facilities for a number of WCAs. Before the changes brought about by the EPA, local authority waste disposal operations were seen as being essentially fixed cost in nature. This annual fixed cost incurred, for example by a county council, was then recovered from the householders within each individual WCA, normally on the basis of the number of people living within each district or borough. This had the effect of every householder having to pay the same amount of money through the then rating system, irrespective of the amount of waste sent for disposal.

The waste disposal contracts which are now being let under the provisions of the EPA are in the majority of cases based on a price per tonne for every tonne of waste sent for disposal rather than being a fixed annual fee. In addition, because the majority of such contracts require the waste being delivered to be weighed, in order to calculate the charges for disposal, it should be possible in future to record the actual tonnage of waste sent for disposal by each individual WCA. The residents of each district or borough could then be charged the average cost of disposal of their own district or borough's waste, rather than the cost being a nominal figure based on population. Within each district or borough, it will still be the case that every household within a given council tax band will pay the same for waste disposal, irrespective of the amount of waste generated.

In North America and Europe there are payment systems which charge householders for both waste collection and waste disposal, on the basis of the amount of waste set out for collection. While such systems can and do encourage waste minimisation and recycling, they also encourage less scrupulous residents to find alternative methods of waste disposal, such as putting their waste into a neighbour's bin or fly-tipping. No such systems have been tried in the UK and indeed could not be introduced without changes in the legislation governing local authority waste collection and disposal.

The use of such direct charging systems as an economic instrument to encourage recycling and waste minimisation has been considered by the government. In the report of the study[13] carried to examine the options available, it was concluded that while it is not possible to predict with any certainty the effects of such charges, their introduction could lead to increases in recycling, provided that appropriate recycling facilities were in place (these would have to be kerbside type facilities). It was also expected that both unauthorised tipping and home incineration (such as bonfires) may increase and in proportion to the level of the charge.

Recycling credits

As the levels of WCA recycling have increased, a situation arose in the late 1980s whereby district and borough councils were incurring the expense of recycling, but it was the associated county council which was receiving any financial benefit of such recycling through the reduction of waste disposal tonnages. A provision was therefore included in the EPA under Section 52(1) which requires waste disposal authorities to make payments to waste collection authorities to reflect any savings in waste disposal costs to the WDA as a result of WCA recycling activities. Section 52(3) confers the same power on WDAs to make similar payments to persons other than WCAs, although this is not obligatory. These sections of the EPA were enacted on 1 April 1992 by the Environmental Protection (Waste Recycling Payments) Regulations 1992. These regulations defined the level of payment to be made as being equivalent to one half of the cost of the most expensive method of waste disposal used by the WDA. The method of calculating waste disposal costs for the purposes of such payments was also set down in the regulations. If a WDA was unable to calculate its disposal costs, a table of typical charges was included in the regulations which ranged from £8 per tonne for shire counties (with a minimum recycling credit of £4.50) to £16 per tonne for London boroughs using waste transfer methods.

The introduction of recycling credits had an immediate and positive impact on the levels of local authority recycling, since from a district or borough perspective a new source of funding was available to support local recycling initiatives.

From 1 April 1994 the calculation of recycling credits is no longer based on 50 per cent of the most expensive method of waste disposal available to the WDA, but rather the full cost of waste disposal, taken as an average of the different methods of disposal used by the WDA. This will increase the level of recycling credits, but will clearly not result in them doubling.

The issue of recycling credits has been a contentious one since its introduction and while it should be seen as a successful measure in terms of correcting an imbalance associated with recycling between district and county councils, it has inevitably led to debate and dissent when the exact methods of calculating recycling credits are considered. For example, with the latest change, the level of credit paid to a district council will be based on the average cost of disposal to the WDA. If a particular district council currently sends its waste to the most expensive disposal point within a county and by recycling is able to reduce the amount of waste being sent for disposal, that district council may well feel that the level of recycling credit payable does not reflect the full waste disposal saving arising to the county.

Section 52(3) of the EPA places a duty on WCAs to pay recycling credits to the WDA if the WDA, through its own recycling activities, reduces the amount of waste to be collected by the WCA, for example, if the WDA provided recycling collection containers at its civic amenity sites. Such payments are likely to be small and the method of calculation is not prescribed, but the Department of the Environment has recommended 70p per tonne as a minimum. However, since this section of the EPA has not yet been exacted, the duty on WCAs to make such payments is not yet in force. Section 52(4) confers the power of WCAs to make similar payments to third parties other than the WDA, but this has also not yet been exacted.

Waste recycling plans

The requirement for waste collection authorities to prepare a waste recycling plan was introduced under Section 49 of the EPA, which requires waste collection authorities to:

- carry out an investigation with a view to deciding what arrangements are appropriate for dealing with the waste by separating, baling or otherwise packaging it for the purpose of recycling it;
- decide what arrangements are in the opinion of the authority needed for that purpose;
- prepare a statement ('the plan') of the arrangements made and proposed to be made by the authority and other persons for dealing with waste in these ways;
- carry out from time to time further investigations with a view to deciding what changes in the plan are needed; and
- make any modification of the plan which the authority thinks appropriate in consequences of any such investigation.

In order to assist local authorities in preparing their plans, the Department of the Environment published Waste Management Paper No 28 – Recycling.[14] This set out the background to the introduction for waste recycling plans, presented a suggested plan structure and approach to its preparation and provided information on the state-of-the-art of recycling at that time.

The EPA set no deadline by which such plans were to be prepared, nor how frequently they were to be reviewed. To ensure that all authorities fulfilled this duty, the Department of the Environment requested that all plans be submitted to the department by 1 August 1992. Each plan was then reviewed to ensure that it had met the legal requirements summarised above.

The review of each plan carried out by the Department of the Environment was limited to ensuring legislative compliance. No check was made as to whether each authority was planning to meet the government's recycling target (as was mistakenly believed by many authorities), nor was any statistical analysis carried out or data extracted from the plans. The review did, however, highlight the fact that many plans contained information which could be of use to other authorities (for example, in the design or operation of recycling schemes) and to other interested parties. The Department of the Environment therefore commissioned a survey of all English recycling plans to extract such useful data and to publicise examples of best practice. This survey was carried out by Coopers & Lybrand and the survey report published in February 1994.[15]

The survey provided many interesting insights into how local authorities viewed recycling and its future development. For example, the variation in the seriousness with which local authorities approached recycling was demonstrated by the range in the length of the plans submitted: from two pages in length to 200 (with an average of 43 pages). Seventy-seven per cent of the plans surveyed set a target for recycling, but 10 per cent did not set a date for its achievement and 39 per cent of the plans committed the authority to meeting or exceeding the government's recycling target. In the majority of cases however, the plans did not provide details of how the stated target was to be achieved, so that such targets were interpreted as a statement of intent rather than as planned figures. The four materials most frequently collected for recycling were:

- glass (91 per cent of authorities);
- paper (81 per cent);
- textiles (67 per cent); and
- metal cans (60 per cent).

Other materials collected included plastics, oil, organic material, cardboard and even Christmas trees. The average reported recycling rate was 3.4 per cent, however, the authors of the report calculated each authority's recycling rate on a standard basis and concluded that a more accurate average recycling rate was about 4.7 per cent.

The overall conclusion of the survey was that the format and methods of data calculation used by different authorities when preparing their recycling plans varied widely. This made it very difficult to generate standardised and consistent data, thus limiting the ability of local authorities and other interested parties to learn from the experience of others. This is another example of a problem that has plagued the development of recycling and not only in the UK. The lack of standards for the preparation of performance data inhibits a rigorous analysis of any recycling scheme and prevents comparison between schemes. Moves to address this problem are, however, in place and are discussed in Chapters 9 and 10.

The requirement to prepare, and the content of many, recycling plans provides us with a useful summary of the state of the development of recycling in 1992:

1) the government had given local authorities and in particular waste collection authorities, a major responsibility for developing recycling;
2) the government had set a national target for recycling which many local authorities had accepted as their own target, but the majority of whom were unable to demonstrate how such a target could be achieved;
3) the plans highlighted the very poor state of available information on all aspects of waste management, identifying an absence of a stable base of data from which to plan developments; and
4) the plans demonstrated how recycling was being seen almost as a peripheral activity, divorced from the other two waste management functions of waste collection and disposal.

This latter point was in part as a result of the involvement of different tiers of local government in different aspects of waste management, as described earlier in this chapter, and partly due to the fact that in many cases recycling was not being taken seriously as a viable alternative form of waste treatment. It is clear that in the majority of local authorities recycling is a cinderella activity.

In the following chapter we will examine those elements of household waste which could potentially be recycled and move on in Chapters 4, 5 and 6 to examine why recycling is a viable waste treatment method and how it could be implemented by local authorities.

CHAPTER THREE

WHAT CAN BE RECYCLED?

———————◆———————

Before we can decide how we can increase the current level of recycling, we need to know what materials there are in the household waste stream which are capable of being recycled and for each of these materials, how much is available. As indicated in Chapter 1, there is very little reliable data available on the amount of waste arising. There is, however, quite detailed information available on the composition of household waste. Such waste is collected both directly from the household in the form of 'dustbin' waste and indirectly through householders taking their waste to civic amenity sites. Household waste also includes bulky waste which is collected from households as a special service, street sweepings and litter. It has been estimated[14] that of the 20m tonnes per annum of household waste, 3–5 million tonnes is civic amenity site waste (approximately 20 per cent of the total). The composition of dustbin waste and civic amenity site waste is very different, as shown in Tables 3.1[16] and 3.2.[17]

The analysis of household waste composition is normally done on the basis of weight. Much of this work has been carried out by the Warren Spring Laboratory and in the absence of any local information, the national average figures shown in Table 3.1 are normally used. This data should, however, be used with care. Not only does the level and composition of waste arising vary with geographic location and socioeconomic factors, but there are also seasonal variations, particularly with regard to garden waste, as indicated in Table 3.2. It is possible to carry out a local waste analysis in order to establish both the levels and the composition of waste arisings, but this is an expensive exercise. In order to generate representative data, samples of waste must be taken from a number of different and representative sites

Table 3.1 Analysis of household waste (dustbin waste)

Material	Percentage by weight			Type or grade	Per cent by weight
	Min	Max	Typical		
Paper and board	21.6	54.1	33.2	Newspapers	11.4
				Magazines	4.6
				Other paper	9.5
				Liquid containers	0.6
				Board packaging	3.8
				Other board	3.1
Plastic film	3.4	8.1	5.3	Refuse sacks	1.2
				Other	4.1
Dense plastic	2.7	10.1	5.9	Clear beverage bottles	0.6
				Coloured beverage bottles	0.1
				Other plastic bottles	1.1
				Food packaging	1.9
				Other	2.1
Glass	2.7	16.9	9.3	Brown glass	1.3
				Green glass	2.4
				Clear glass	5.4
				Other	0.2
Ferrous metal	2.8	10.8	5.7	Beverage cans	0.5
				Food cans	3.7
				Batteries	0.1
				Other cans	0.4
				Other	1.0
Non-ferrous metal	0.3	3.9	1.6	Beverage cans	0.4
				Foil	0.5
				Other	0.7
Textiles	1.1	3.4	2.1		2.1
Putrescibles	13.9	27.8	20.2	Garden waste	3.4
				Other	16.8
Miscellaneous combustibles	1.4	13.6	8.1	Disposable nappies	4.2
				Other	3.9
Miscellaneous non-combustibles	0.4	4.2	1.8		1.8
Fines	3.5	12.4	6.8		6.8
TOTAL			100.0		100.0

Table 3.2 Analysis of household waste (civic amenity site waste)

Material	Percentage by weight	
	January	May
Paper and board	5.7	2.2
Plastics	0.7	1.8
Glass	1.8	0.7
Metal	14.8	2.8
Textiles	5.2	2.1
Wood	10.9	4.1
Garden waste – small	18.2	54.6
Garden waste – large[1]	3.7	9.2
Oil	1.9	0.0
Large household items[2]	5.2	8.8
Miscellaneous combustibles	4.2	1.4
Miscellaneous non-combustibles	23.0	9.1
Bagged household waste	4.7	4.8
TOTAL	100.0	100.0

1 defined as being over 450mm, for example tree branches; 2 defined as being over 450mm, for example furniture and white goods

in the area being considered, and such samples should be taken periodically over at least a three month period, but preferably over a twelve month period.

Clearly it is very important to know what materials are present in the waste stream and in what proportions, before any plans are made to introduce recycling, but as indicated above, such information is often not available at a local level. The government has recognised the problems associated with establishing this information, and in 1991 set up a project called the National Household Waste Analysis Project to generate data on the composition and weight of household waste. The objectives of this project are to generate data which is representative of the UK as a whole and to develop a capability to predict the composition and weight of waste arisings at a local level. The project has developed an approach which will use census data to allocate well defined groups of households (enumeration groups) to the relevant ACORN (A Classification of Residential Neighbourhood) groups. Five tonne samples of household waste from collection rounds which are representative of each of the ACORN groups have been analysed for both weight and composition. These samples will then be used as the basis for predicting household waste arisings at any local and at a national level. The project will not be completed for some time; results from the first stage of Phase 2 of the project were published in August 1994.[18] Sufficient data has however been generated for predictions to be made of the level and composition of arisings for any local authority.

The recyclable materials within household waste fall into three broad categories:

1) dry recyclables – paper, cardboard, glass, plastics, metals and textiles;
2) organic material – kitchen or food waste and garden waste; and
3) miscellaneous materials – for example furniture and white goods.

Table 3.3 The recyclability of household waste (dustbin waste)

Material	Percentage by weight[1]	Percentage by volume[2]	Percentage by weight[3] Recyclable	Non-recyclable
Paper and board	33.2	40.0	16.0	17.3
Plastic film	5.3	13.6		5.3
Dense plastic	5.9	12.1	1.9	4.0
Glass	9.3	1.5	9.1	0.2
Ferrous metal	5.7	15.2	4.3	1.3
Non-ferrous metal	1.6	1.5	0.4	1.3
Textiles	2.1	1.2		2.1
Dry recyclables sub-total	*63.1*	*85.1*	*31.7*	*31.5*
Putrescibles	20.2	6.0	20.2	
Miscellaneous combustibles	8.1	7.6		8.1
Miscellaneous non-combustibles	1.8	0.3		1.8
Fines	6.8	1.5		6.8
TOTAL	*100.0*	*100.0*	*57.9*	*48.1*

Sources: 1 Warren Spring Laboratory[16]; 2 calculated from (1) and estimates of material bulk densities; 3 Warren Spring Laboratory[16]

Other materials such as oil, waste paint and batteries are also collected ostensibly for recycling, but in some instances such collection is in fact for safe disposal rather than for recycling.

In terms of composition, Table 3.3 shows that the dry recyclables make up approximately 63 per cent by weight and 85 per cent by volume of the average dustbin. Organic waste accounts for a further 20 per cent by weight, and only 6 per cent by volume of dustbin waste, but can represent as much as 55–65 per cent of household civic amenity site waste.

Table 3.3 also presents a summary of work done by Warren Spring Laboratory to estimate how much of the waste materials in a typical dustbin could be recycled. This work suggests that a little over one half of all such waste is recyclable, a figure which supports the government's target of recycling one half of the recyclable fraction of household waste, that is, 25 per cent of the total.

There are, however, some anomalies in this data:

■ all newspapers and magazines are presented as being recyclable, but all board packaging and other board grades are considered to be non-recyclable;
■ all plastic film is recorded as being non-recyclable, as is all plastic food packaging;
■ metal cans other than beverage and food cans are classed as non-recyclable;
■ aluminium foil is excluded from the recyclable category; and
■ all textiles are considered non-recyclable.

All of these materials are potentially recyclable[19] and if these materials are included in the recyclable fraction, the recyclable proportion of dustbin waste is increased to 71 per cent.

However, not all of this material can be recycled in practice, for a number of reasons:

■ some material is too contaminated, in particular by food waste;
■ some material exists as mixed products, for example composite packaging, and therefore could not be recycled as individual materials;
■ some items are physically too small to be economically separated at a sorting plant; or
■ even though the material can be separated, there is no viable market for it.

It is these factors which have been taken into account by Warren Spring Laboratory when determining the recyclability of the materials shown in Table 3.3. However, the exclusion of all board (6.9 per cent of total arisings), all plastic film (5.3 per cent), all dense plastic except bottles (4 per cent), steel cans other than beverage and food cans (0.4 per cent), aluminium foil (0.5 per cent) and textiles (2.1 per cent) is not fully justified. Certainly some of the board, plastic and aluminium foil food packaging will be too contaminated to recycle and the markets for plastic film, given its low bulk density, are not good. A proportion of these materials should therefore be classed as non-recyclable. Equally, not all newspapers and magazines will be recyclable due to contamination, not all glass, due to breakage; and not all plastic bottles, due to contamination and poor polymer separation. The classification of materials in Table 3.3 is therefore too simplistic, but serves to highlight the problem of trying to establish how much material is potentially recyclable.

An alternative approach is shown in Table 3.4. This shows estimates of how much of each material category is available as 'clean' material in the waste stream and takes no account of whether a market for the material exists or not. This shows that 62 per cent of the dustbin waste is potentially recyclable. Two-thirds of this figure (42 per cent of the total) is derived from dry recyclables, the remainder from organic waste.

Given the comments above regarding the theoretical maximum of 71 per cent of dustbin waste being potentially recyclable, the figure of 62 per cent as the limit of practical recyclability would appear reasonable. This figure supports the government's target of recycling 25 per cent of all household waste, or 50 per cent of the recyclable fraction, since 62 per cent of dustbin waste equates approximately to 50 per cent of household waste.

We therefore have a practical target to aim at, that is, to recycle 62 per cent of household dustbin waste stream. One-third of this recyclable material is paper and board, one-third is organic material and the remaining third is made up of approximately equal proportions of plastic, glass and metals and a small proportion of textiles. These proportions are extremely important and are a major consideration when designing a recycling scheme, in terms of the selection of the methods of collection, processing and reprocessing.

It is also important to note the very low percentage of materials which have any

Table 3.4 The recyclability of household waste (dustbin waste)

Material	Percentage by weight (A)	Clean material as a percentage of (A)[20]	Clean material as a percentage of total waste
Paper and board	33.2	60.0	19.9
Plastic film	5.3	60.0	3.2
Dense plastic	5.9	70.0	4.1
Glass	9.3	90.0	8.4
Ferrous metal	5.7	80.0	4.6
Aluminium	1.6	70.0	1.1
Textiles	2.1	50.0	1.1
Dry recyclables sub-total	63.1		42.4
Putrescibles and other	36.9		20.2
TOTAL	100.0		62.2

real monetary value. Of the materials listed in Table 3.4, only glass and aluminium have any real monetary value and represent less than 10 per cent of dustbin waste if recycled. This shows why it is a fallacy to believe that recycling can pay for itself, let alone make a profit. The majority of the materials that are recyclable have little or no monetary value. However, as set out in Chapter 1, recycling is not about making money.

In conclusion, 62 per cent of dustbin waste could be recycled or converted back into a material form, but it should be noted that two-thirds of this figure is made up of organic material (putrescibles plus paper and board) which could equally be composted to produce a soil conditioning product.

Having identified how much of the waste stream is recyclable, we now need to consider what are the most appropriate methods for treating our household waste. In order to do this we start in the next chapter by examining exactly what the options are for waste management.

CHAPTER FOUR

WASTE MANAGEMENT OPTIONS

———————— ◆ ————————

In the previous chapter we identified those materials in the household waste stream which are potentially recyclable. In order to realise this potential, the existing methods of waste collection need to be changed and new techniques of material separation need to be implemented. However, as we have seen, not all waste is recyclable, so that there will be a continuing need for the existing refuse collection and disposal services. It is therefore vital that any new arrangements for recycling are integrated with the existing methods of refuse collection and disposal, in order to ensure that we maximise the efficiency and effectiveness of both methods of waste management. It is hoped that the long-awaited National Waste Strategy,[8] which is to be developed during 1995, will actively support such integration.

In the next three chapters we will consider in detail the arrangements necessary for achieving recycling, but in order to understand the context within which these need to be developed, we will begin by examining the existing methods and options for waste collection and waste disposal.

Waste collection

Waste collection authorities (WCAs) are responsible for the collection of household waste from individual households. Each WCA must provide a regular collection service to householders, but is able to choose the type of container to be provided (either by the WCA or by the householder) and the frequency of collection. The survey of local authority recycling plans carried out by Coopers &

Lybrand for the Department of the Environment in 1993[18] reported the following usage of refuse collection container types:

- refuse sacks (48 per cent);
- wheeled bins (25 per cent);
- traditional dustbins (27 per cent).

The frequency of collection is normally weekly, although in urban areas of high housing density this may be twice weekly and in rural areas collection may be fortnightly.

Until the late 1980s, the vast majority of household waste collection was carried out by each local authority's own Direct Service Organisation (DSO). However, the 1988 Local Government Act introduced a requirement for the compulsory competitive tendering of such services. Under CCT a contract for the provision of such services must be offered regularly for open competition by the WCA, thus allowing private sector companies to tender for such work. While many DSOs have successfully tendered for and won their own authority's contract, an increasing number of contracts are being awarded to private sector companies.

The vehicles used to collect household refuse have become increasingly sophisticated and are known collectively as refuse collection vehicles (RCVs). Most RCVs are rear-end loaders (RELs), that is, the refuse is loaded into the rear of the vehicle (an example is shown in Figure 4.1). In order to maximise the payload

Figure 4.1 A standard refuse collection vehicle

Reproduced by kind permission of Haller UK Limited

of the vehicle and hence its collection efficiency, all such vehicles have compaction devices which compress the loose refuse, normally in a ratio of about 3:1. Such compaction is usually achieved by a simple hydraulic ram system, but one variant uses a rotating drum within the vehicle body to compact the waste using a screw action. When an RCV is full, it is driven to the point of discharge (a landfill site, incinerator or transfer station), the rear section of the vehicle body is raised and the compacted refuse ejected using the hydraulic ram which forms part of the compaction system (see Figure 4.2). A very important point to bear in mind when designing a facility in which RCVs will discharge their collected load, for example in a materials recovery facility (MRF), is the internal roof height needed to provide clearance for the vehicle to discharge.

The type of refuse collection container and the arrangements for its collection determine the size of the collection vehicle crew required. For example, a collection system based on refuse sacks being collected by the crew from the rear of a household (called 'back-door' collection) will typically require a crew of four or five operators plus a driver, while a collection scheme based on the provision of wheeled bins which are set out at the kerbside by the householder will typically require a vehicle with a crew of only two plus a driver.

The costs of refuse collection vary considerably with the methods used and the area being serviced. Costs as low as £15 per tonne have been reported for an urban area where householders are limited to setting out one refuse sack per week at the kerbside, to £45 per tonne for a wheeled bin based system including garden waste.

Figure 4.2 A refuse collection vehicle discharging

Reproduced by kind permission of Haller UK Limited

Collection costs are clearly higher for rural areas where the collection vehicle spends a greater proportion of its time travelling between pick-up points.

Collection round sizes vary with the method of collection employed and the nature of the area being serviced. The Coopers & Lybrand survey of recycling plans[22] identified a reported range of 1000–9000 households per round with the average being 4764.

Waste disposal

The predominant method of waste disposal in this country has been and remains landfill. This is as a result of the geological makeup of our island, which has provided us with an active and large scale mineral extraction industry resulting in the creation of a large number of holes in the ground which we can fill with waste. Not only have we created these holes, but the underlying geology, either in terms of the rock formation or clay deposits, has in many cases made these holes suitable for use as landfill sites. The great availability of potential sites and the ease (in many cases) with which they can be prepared for landfilling, has resulted in landfilling being an inexpensive and widespread activity in this country.

New legislation and regulations, for example the draft EU Directive on Landfill (93/C212/02) are now placing much more onerous conditions on the operators of landfill sites in order to improve the standards to which such sites are operated, and hence their environmental performance. This will result in the costs of landfill rising significantly (a process which has already started). Such legislation and regulations primarily address the five key aspects of operating a landfill site:

1) the need to provide a permanent and impermeable lining to the site in order to contain the waste and to prevent any migration of the deposited material into the surrounding environment;

2) the need to provide methods of collecting, treating and disposing of the liquid leachate with arises within a landfill site and which can be potentially toxic in nature and which must be prevented from entering into any surrounding water sources;

3) the need to control methane gas which is generated within landfill sites as a result of the anaerobic decomposition of organic materials, either by collection and flaring or by collection and use as a fuel;

4) at the end of the active life of the site, the need to provide appropriate capping and landscape restoration, both to seal the site and to return the land for alternative uses; and

5) both during the life of a site and following its closure, the need to provide continuous and effective monitoring to detect any solid, liquid or gaseous emissions from the site.

The costs of landfill will be further increased when the landfill tax announced in the September 1994 budget is introduced in April 1996.

The regulatory requirements on operators of landfill sites are becoming more onerous and the techniques and operating practices of landfilling are becoming more sophisticated. The investment and skill required to develop new sites is thus increasing, and has resulted in a move away from large numbers of small local landfill sites serving individual communities towards far fewer, much larger landfill sites serving larger populations and inevitably requiring waste to be transported longer distances in order to reach its final destination. This change has been accompanied by a dramatic rationalisation of the companies involved in landfilling operations. This has seen the majority of small companies either going out of business or being taken over by an increasingly small number of large and professional waste management companies.

Waste disposal sites are divided into a series of cells which are filled one at a time as part of the construction and control of the site. As waste is deposited each day it is covered with a layer of soil or other inert material such as construction waste, in order to minimise nuisance from windblown litter, odours and vermin. Such inert material is called 'landfill cover' and some wastes, such as building rubble, are often accepted at landfill sites either free of charge or are even paid for, because of the large demand that such sites have for this material. The heavy bulldozer-like compactor vehicles which are used to move the waste around the site are specifically designed to compact the waste as they drive over it, in order to maximise the amount of waste disposed of in the site. The lining, leachate treatment and gas control features of a modern landfill site are illustrated in Figure 4.3.

Landfill gas

Landfill gas is a mixture of methane and carbon dioxide which is generated within landfill sites and which has historically been a problem, since the gas seeps out and is combustible. The production of such gas has therefore been a problem to be controlled, but is increasingly being seen as an opportunity. Given that such gas must be collected in order to prevent its seepage, such collection results in the supply of a combustible fuel source. This fuel has been put to good effect, for example at a number of sites in Buckinghamshire where the gas is supplied to adjacent cement kilns for firing the cement production process, or increasingly where sufficient quantities are produced, small scale gas turbine driven generators are being installed to produce electrical power which is then fed into the National Grid.

Incineration

The alternative method of waste disposal to landfill is that of waste incineration. Waste incinerators use the process of combustion to convert many of the materials within household waste into their primary components of water, carbon dioxide and carbon. Clearly not all household waste materials are combustible, for example metals and glass, so that following combustion a solid waste residue remains to be disposed of and this residue is normally sent to landfill. Incineration should therefore be seen as a means of reducing the amount of waste to be disposed of by landfill, rather than a method of ultimate disposal in its own right.

Incineration became a popular method of waste treatment in the 1960s and

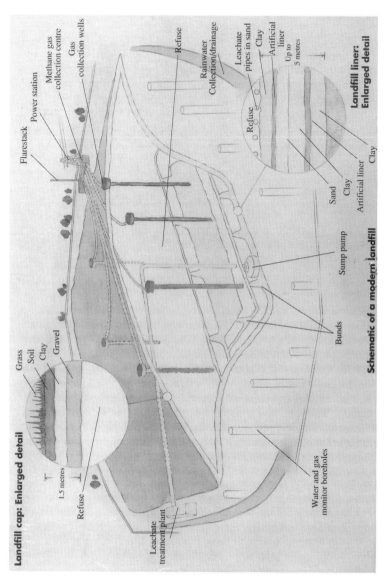

Figure 4.3 Typical features of a modern landfilled site

Reproduced by kind permission of Biffa Waste Services Ltd

1970s when many incinerators were constructed, but increasing concerns over the emissions from such plants resulted in a reduction in their popularity from the late 1970s onwards (only one incinerator has been build since 1979[23]). The two EC Directives on emissions from waste incinerators introduced in 1989 (89/429/EEC for existing municipal incinerators and 89/369/EEC for new municipal incinerators) will come into force in 1995 and 1996 and will set much tougher standards for the levels of emissions which such incinerators will be allowed to produce. As a result, all but a handful of the thirty municipal waste incinerators currently operating in the UK are expected to close between 1995 and 1996, since they will be unable to meet these new emission standards. Those incinerators which continue to operate after 1995 will have to have expensive emission control equipment fitted in order for them to meet the new standards.

The tightening of air emission standards is to be welcomed, although the new incinerators which are planned or under construction, or those existing incinerators which will continue to operate after 1995/96, will still produce high levels of airborne emissions. The plants will be fitted with equipment such as flue gas scrubbers, which remove the majority of such airborne material, before it is exhausted from the plant. However this material, once removed, must still be disposed of. This solid waste, known as 'fly-ash', is by its very nature toxic (and as emission standards increase, will become more so) and can only be disposed of by landfilling, so that we are in effect moving the problem, not eliminating it.

There has always been a significant level of public concern regarding the airborne emissions from municipal waste incinerators. As a result of the implementation of new standards from Her Majesty's Inspectorate of Pollution (HMIP) which implement the EC directives mentioned above, the levels of such emissions will be substantially reduced. However, while acknowledging this, the Royal Commission on Environmental Pollution in their Seventeenth Report on the Incineration of Waste, made the following points and recommendations:

- for most pollutants, existing municipal waste incinerators produce a small or negligible proportion of total UK emissions (with the exception of mercury for which the reduction in emissions may only be marginal and for cadmium for which the reduction may only be one half), and even with a large increase in the amount of such waste being incinerated, provided such incinerations meet the new HMIP standards, the emissions from such plants would not be a cause for concern;[24]
- the evidence is that the emissions from well operated waste incinerators which comply with the new HMIP standards are most unlikely to cause any health effects; however, despite this conclusion the Commission believes that there are some further measures which ought to be taken to reduce emissions from incinerators and the risk that heavy metals from solid residues will leach into ground water;[25]
- further reductions should be sought in the emissions of heavy metals, which is likely to require recycling schemes or other actions to remove them from the waste stream prior to incineration, and there is also a case for tightening the new HMIP standards for hydrogen fluoride, sulphur dioxide and nitrogen

oxides, although municipal incineration plants produce only a small proportion of the UK emissions of these gases;[26]

■ the Commission recommended that rather than continuing to include it with other metals, HMIP should set a separate standard for emissions of lead to air from incineration plants;[27]

■ with regard to public concern over incinerator emissions, the Commission made two recommendations:[28]

– that the waste management industry should adopt a policy of openness in providing information to the public, identify the best practices in that respect and take care to apply these generally; and

– that there should be a requirement on the operator of a plant to disclose information about the chemical composition of wastes incinerated, except where there is a genuine issue of security or commercial confidentiality affecting the customers sending waste for disposal.

It is clear therefore that the new generation of incinerators and those existing plants which continue to operate after 1995/96, will generate much lower levels of airborne emissions. However, even the Royal Commission on Environmental Pollution has not given such plants a completely clean bill of health, and while even these reduced levels of concern over emissions exist, there will continue to be a strong public resistance to the incineration of waste.

During the early 1990s there was a renewed interest in incineration, particularly in the form of waste to energy (see below). However, the publication in 1994 of a report by the US Environmental Protection Agency which appeared to link dioxin emissions from incineration with cancer in humans rekindled public anxiety regarding this method of waste treatment.[29]

Apart from airborne emissions, another area of environmental concern regarding the incineration of waste is the contribution that such plants make to global warming. The incineration of waste produces large quantities of carbon dioxide (a so-called greenhouse gas). The Royal Commission on Environmental Pollution presented data in their seventeenth report[30] to show that if all of the UK's municipal waste was incinerated, the carbon dioxide generated would equate to approximately four per cent of the total UK greenhouse gas emissions.

By way of comparison, the landfilling of waste generates both carbon dioxide and methane (a much more damaging greenhouse gas). Recent estimates[30] suggest that the landfilling of waste contributes approximately one half of the total UK emissions of methane (the other major contributor being ruminating farm animals), and six per cent of total UK greenhouse gas emissions. Such is the impact of methane that the Royal Commission estimated that if all municipal waste were to be incinerated rather than landfilled, there would be a net reduction in UK greenhouse gas emissions of approximately five per cent.

Waste to energy plants

The combustion of waste in an incinerator obviously generates heat. While in the majority of incinerators in this country, this heat is simply vented to the atmosphere, a number of plants make use of this heat either to provide steam to surrounding buildings as a heat source (often described as a district heating scheme) or increasingly, to provide steam for the generation of electrical power using steam turbine generators. Where an incinerator makes use of the heat generated by combustion, it is called a waste to energy (WTE) plant. Where the waste heat is used for both heating and the generation of electrical power, this is described as a combined heat and power (CHP) scheme. This is clearly one way in which the energy content of waste materials can be recovered and is infinitely preferable to simply burning refuse.

Very few of the present generation of incinerators were built with the intention to recover energy. However, this situation changed as a result of a provision within the Electricity Bill of 1989 which created the non-fossil fuel obligation (NFFO). This requires the newly privatised power generators to pay a premium for any electricity generated from non-fossil fuel sources, such as household waste. The NFFO subsidy has changed the economics of WTE plants to such an extent that they are now an attractive commercial proposition which, as landfill prices continue to rise, can compete more successfully with the alternative of landfill. This has resulted in proposals for a number of modern WTE plants, capable of meeting the new EC emission standards and generating electrical power in significant quantities.

It is significant however, that all such proposals are for energy recovery in the form of electrical power only, since the NFFO subsidy does not apply to heat generation. While it is clear that progress has been made in encouraging the recovery of energy from waste, more needs to be done. The thermal efficiency of a WTE incinerator generating electricity is in the range 20–25 per cent, whereas the figure for an CHP incinerator is of the order of 50–60 per cent. These figures should be compared with that of a coal-fired power station of 38–40 per cent. Clearly, to maximise the environmental benefit, WTE incinerators should generate both heat and power, so why are so few CHP schemes in existence or planned? Apart from the absence of the NFFO subsidy for heat recovery, one of the reasons that so few district heating schemes exist in this country is the problem of creating the necessary stream distribution infrastructure to take the waste heat from an incinerator to surrounding buildings. For example, the district heating scheme which is fed by the Eastcroft incinerator in Nottingham was only possible because the steam mains required to transfer the heat could be laid along disused rail tracks in the city centre. The costs of creating such a piping network underground would have been prohibitive. The new SELCHP (South East London Combined Heat and Power) WTE plant will only generate power for the foreseeable future, since the cost of installing the steam main to transfer heat out of the plant, together with the reduction in the NFFO subsidy income as a result of generating heat (a small proportion of the power generation capacity would be lost) makes heat generation financially unattractive.

Refuse derived fuel

Following the development of waste incinerators, it was natural for attention to be turned to the possibility of using refuse as a fuel in other combustion equipment, such as industrial boilers. Clearly such equipment is not designed to accept raw refuse as a fuel stock, so that techniques were developed to convert refuse into a more usable form known as refuse derived fuel (RDF). Various techniques have been developed which convert part of the waste stream, once certain elements have been removed, to produce a dry fuel in pellet form which can be used in a wide range of combustion equipment. The two key elements of such processes are the drying of the refuse to reduce its water content and converting the refuse into pellets to provide a fuel form which can be readily handled. Items which may be removed from the waste prior to RDF production include metals, glass and organic material, although with some techniques this latter category remains in the RDF.

The logic of RDF production is sound, provided that the energy used to produce the fuel is less than the additional energy available in the fuel as a result of processing compared with the energy of the raw waste. However, RDF has not become established as an alternative fuel source, and has not proved to be as attractive to commercial users as was originally anticipated. This is partly due to:

- problems with handling the material;
- the relative costs of RDF compared to other fuel sources (taking into account the relative calorific value of RDF); and
- concerns over the emissions from combustion equipment burning RDF.

Indeed, in their 17th Report, the Royal Commission on Environmental Pollution recommended that the HMIP standards for emissions to air from combustion processes, particularly those using waste as a fuel, should be re-examined to see whether they should be brought more closely in to line with the new HMIP standards for incineration.[31]

One type of RDF plant which was developed took raw refuse and using a series of screening and separation processes, produced two products: RDF, which was rich in paper and plastics, and an organic rich fraction which was composted to produce a soil conditioner. An example of such a plant was that operated by Secondary Resources Limited in Birmingham, but which closed in 1992.

There is now a renewed interest in producing a high calorific value fuel from waste, but not in the same way that RDF is produced. The new approach recognises that recycling markets for paper, board and plastics may be limited and proposes the production of a pelletised fuel produced from source-separated paper, board and plastics. Such an approach has the advantage of producing a fuel with a known composition, a high calorific value and which is relatively free of materials which are known to give rise to emission problems.

Material recycling

Having considered the options for waste disposal and energy recovery we will now turn our attention to the alternative method of waste management, that of recycling.

For the purposes of recycling, the household waste stream can be divided into two categories:

1) **dry recyclables**, comprising paper, plastics, metals, glass and textiles; and
2) **organics**, consisting of both kitchen (food) and garden waste.

Both categories of material may be recycled as material, but the methods of collection and treatment are quite different. This is a subject that we will examine in more detail in later chapters, however we will present a summary here.

Dry recyclable materials can be separated either at source, that is by the householder, into individual materials for collection and subsequent reprocessing, or they can be collected as a mixture of materials (termed *commingled collection*). There are various methods of effecting such collection, but the point that they have in common is that the commingled materials require separation into individual materials following collection from the household. This separation is carried out in a materials recovery facility or MRF (the American term for a sorting plant) and uses manual, semi-automatic or automatic separation methods. This sorting operation is then followed by material reprocessing.

Following collection, organic material can be treated in one of two ways:

1) **Composting:** this simple method of treatment is a process by which the material undergoes a controlled, natural decomposition to produce a dry, odourless and friable organic material, which is suitable for a variety of soil conditioning uses.
2) **Anaerobic digestion**, a technique in which the material again undergoes a natural process of decomposition, but in this case in the absence of oxygen. The process produces methane gas as a product of the decomposition, and such gas is collected for use as a fuel source. Following digestion, the digestate is subjected to a process of composting in order to stabilise the final product.

In its simplest form composting can be carried out in the open air, the only requirements being a solid base on which to lay out the compost and a leachate control system. The more sophisticated compost techniques take place in an enclosed building and feature full atmospheric control, including odour control. Such techniques are clearly more expensive than the simple open air approach. Anaerobic digestion takes place in a sealed pressure vessel with associated control equipment and is a much more capital intensive process.

The compatibility of recycling with other waste management options

Recycling and waste minimisation and reuse

The linkage between reuse and recycling is a simple one. In order to minimise the environmental impact of any reusable container, it should be recycled at the end of its useful life. The case for recycling discarded reusable containers is stronger than that of single-trip containers, since in order to survive the rigours of multiple trips, the reusable container must be thicker and heavier than its one-way equivalent. The amount of material per container which can be recycled is thus greater. The only issue to be addressed is simply the fact that when designing a reusable container, consideration should be given to how it will be recycled at the end of its useful life.

The relationship between waste minimisation and recycling is less clear and in some instances, recycling may actually appear to discourage waste minimisation. This apparent contradiction stems from the problem of how we define waste minimisation.

In simple terms, waste minimisation is any action which results in a reduction of the amount of waste being generated and is measured in terms of the weight of waste produced. However, such a definition takes no account of the recovery potential of the waste which is produced and suggests that an action to reduce waste which can be recycled is of equal value to one which reduces waste which can only be disposed of.

Let us examine a case in point. As an example, consider a packaging container which currently is very difficult to recycle and is which normally sent for land-filling. We could substitute an alternative packaging material which is recyclable but which, for the same packaging function, is heavier. By making the substitution, according to the above definition, we are doing the opposite of waste minimisation. However, if after recycling, the amount of residue from the alternative container sent to landfill is less than the total of the original container, have we not minimised the overall level of waste? Such an example would be the replacement of a composite drinks carton with a plastic or glass bottle (a highly contentious issue). Clearly, the environmental impact of such a substitution goes beyond the issue of waste generation and would need a full life cycle analysis to determine the correct approach, but the example does serve to demonstrate that the concept of waste minimisation must be treated with care, and that waste minimisation and recycling can be compatible.

A more easily understood relationship between these two issues is the indirect effect that recycling has by simply making consumers aware of the issue of waste. The very tangible action of recycling makes each of us aware of the need for resource conservation and can provide a stimulus to be aware of and reconsider our consumption behaviour. The practical activity of recycling can thus encourage a change in individual attitudes which leads to actions of waste minimisation, such as refusing unnecessary plastic bags in shops, reusing or repairing products which might previously have been discarded or simply reducing our consumption.

Recycling and waste to energy incineration

The discussion of whether it is preferable to recycle or recover energy is often characterised by polarised views which exclusively support one or other option. However, material recycling and energy recovery are not necessarily mutually exclusive methods of waste treatment. The most obvious example of the compatibility of recycling and energy recovery is the magnetic extraction of steel (predominantly steel cans) from mixed refuse, either prior to or after incineration. Clearly the extraction of such cans prior to incineration is preferable since the tinplate coating is preserved for reprocessing (see Chapter 7) and the non-combustible metal is removed prior to combustion, thus improving the calorific value of the remaining refuse. While this is a simple example of how the two methods of waste treatment can be combined, more importantly it is an example of how recycling can significantly improve the energy recovery potential of non-recyclable waste.

Table 4.1 sets out the waste treatment options available for specific materials within the household waste stream. The three methods of recovery which are presented are material recycling, incineration (assuming energy recovery) and composting (or anaerobic digestion). As can be seen from the table, paper and board and natural fibre textiles may be treated by any of these methods, plastics can be recovered by material recycling or WTE incineration and organics by WTE incineration or composting. The only materials for which material recycling is the sole recovery option are metals and glass.

By removing metals and glass from the waste stream prior to energy recovery by incineration, the diversion from landfill can be maximised, since not only can metals and glass only be recovered by materials recycling, but they inhibit energy recovery during incineration. The removal of such material from an incinerator feedstock will therefore improve the energy recovery of that incinerator.

In simplistic terms, the removal of non-combustible materials from an incinerator feedstock will improve its performance, while the diversion of combustible materials such as paper and plastics, for example for material recycling, can reduce the performance of energy recovery by incineration. This effect is demonstrated in Table 4.2, which summarises work undertaken by Warren Spring Laboratory[32] to assess the effect of the diversion of different elements of the household waste stream from an incinerator feedstock.

Referring to Table 4.2, Scheme A is based on a blue box kerbside scheme, and shows that the removal of a large proportion of dry recyclables could achieve a diversion rate of 24 per cent, while only reducing the calorific value of the remaining waste stream by four per cent. Such a small reduction in calorific value demonstrates the trade-off between, in this case, removing a large proportion of the

Table 4.1 Methods of waste treatment

Material	Material recycling	WTE incineration	Composting (digestion)
Paper and board	✓	✓	✓
Textiles	✓	✓	(✓)[1]
Plastics	✓	✓	
Metals	✓		
Glass	✓		
Organics		✓	✓

1 Natural fibre textiles only

Table 4.2 Predicted effect of source separation on the calorific value of waste

Scheme	Waste stream treatment	Diversion rate %	Calorific value of residue MJ/kg
	Mixed refuse	0	9.1
A	Kerbside removal of dry recyclables	24	8.7
B	Kerbside removal of dry recyclables and organics	40	10.4
C	Kerbside removal of organics and bring scheme for cans and glass	39	12.5

non-combustible glass and metal cans, and a relatively smaller percentage of the paper and board and plastic elements of the waste stream. Scheme B, which is based on a green bin kerbside scheme with both dry recyclables and organics being removed, demonstrates a much higher diversion rate at 40 per cent together with a 14 per cent *increase* in calorific value, demonstrating the beneficial effect of removing the wet organic waste from the incinerator feedstock. Scheme C does not remove any of the combustible dry recyclable elements of the waste stream, only the non-combustible metal cans and glass, together with the organic elements of the waste stream. This shows a similar diversion rate to that of Scheme B but with a much greater increase in calorific value of 37 per cent. Thus there is a significant beneficial effect of removing non-combustible and wet elements from the incinerator feedstock prior to energy recovery.

Similar effects are shown in Tables 4.3[33] and Table 4.4,[34] both of which report more specifically the diversion of various materials. In both cases, the diversion of dry recyclables increases the calorific value of the remaining waste, unless plastics are included, in which case the calorific value falls. However, any such fall can be compensated for by the diversion of organic material. Of particular interest is the case in Table 4.4, where 50 per cent of the dry recyclables and 50 per cent of the putrescibles are diverted, a case equating to the government's recycling target. This

Table 4.3 The effect of various recycling programmes upon waste heating values[1]

Percentage of material removed for recycling (%)					Diversion rate (%)	Percentage of calorific value of mixed refuse (%)
Paper	Glass	Metals	Plastics/ textiles	Vegetables		
0	0	0	0	0	0	100[2]
75	80				26	100
75	80	50	40		31	84
75	80		40	94	60	112
50	50			94	47	133

1 Based on German data; 2 calorific value of mixed waste 7.3 MJ/kg

Table 4.4 The effect of recycling on the gross calorific value of household waste

Percentage of material removed for recycling (%)					Diversion rate (%)	Gross calorific value (MJ/kg)
Paper	Glass	Metals	Plastics	Putrescibles		
0	0	0	0	0	0	10.4
10	50				8	10.7
50	50		50		18	9.2
50	50	50	50	50	35	10.8
50	50			50	20	10.4

shows a 35 per cent diversion rate with almost no impact on the calorific value of the remaining waste (less than a four per cent increase).

Tables 4.2, 4.3 and 4.4 suggest that under the right circumstances, far from being mutually exclusive, recycling and energy recovery are at least compatible, if not mutually beneficial.

The successful combination of material recycling and energy recovery is dependent upon which materials are recycled and in what proportion.

Table 4.5 presents a summary of the amount of material which is potentially recyclable in the household waste stream,[35] compared with that which is potentially combustible. These figures take account of the quality of the recyclable material, for example 33 per cent of household waste is made up of paper and board, however, only 20 per cent of the total is shown as being recyclable with the remaining 13 per cent being non-recyclable because of contamination and multi-material combinations such as packaging. This table shows a total potential recyclable element of 52 per cent (which is the approximate basis for the government's recycling target) compared with an overall combustible percentage of 82 per cent.

Table 4.5 suggests that if all of the recyclable material were to be recycled, giving a diversion rate of 52 per cent, a further 46 per cent of the total waste stream would still be suitable for combustion. Alternatively, if only the metals and glass were

Table 4.5 Recycling and energy recovery potential of household waste

Material	Recyclable (%)	Combustible (%)	Non-recyclable but combustible (%)
Paper and board	20	33	13
Textiles	2	4	2
Plastics	4	7	3
Metals	7		
Glass	9		
Organics	10	38	28
TOTAL	52	82	46

recycled, giving a diversion rate of 16 per cent and the remaining waste incinerated, an overall diversion rate again of 98 per cent could be achieved. This poses two questions. First, would the 46 per cent of non-recyclable but combustible waste have a sufficiently high calorific value for viable energy recovery? The discussion of Tables 4.2, 4.3 and 4.4 suggests that this would be the case. Secondly, we are left with the issue of whether the overall recovery rate of 98 per cent would be better achieved by maximising recycling and incineration of the remainder, or by energy recovery from the total waste stream, excluded metals and glass?

The decision as to whether it is better to recycle or to recover energy is dependent on local circumstances as illustrated in Figure 4.4. In simplistic terms, if a particular area has good access to a local WTE incinerator and is distant from recyclable material markets, it would appear to make financial and environmental sense to incinerate all of the available waste in order to recover the energy content. Conversely, where there are strong local markets for recyclable materials and where the density of population would not make incineration viable, for example in a rural area, recycling would appear to be the preferred option. Only where there is equal local access to both recyclable material markets and an appropriate WTE incinerator facility, could the maximum combined recovery rate be achieved, and it is in this case that the dilemma of whether to recycle or recover energy is most acute. This dilemma can at present only be resolved by taking local circumstances into account and making decisions based primarily on practical considerations rather than hard environmental data.

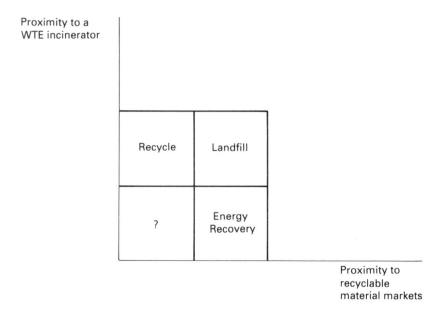

Figure 4.4 Recycling versus energy recovery

Recycling and landfill

Another example of where recycling and waste disposal techniques can be designed to be complimentary is that of combined material sorting and transfer stations. This already happens to a limited extent in very large transfer stations where steel (predominantly in the form of steel cans) is removed from the waste stream by magnetic extraction.

However, the concept can be developed further with regard to source separated recyclables. If large scale recycling, including the centralised processing of recyclables is to be introduced into an area where the method of waste disposal employed includes a waste transfer station for the bulking up of waste, prior to long distance transportation to the point of disposal, significant savings can be made by combining the MRF and transfer station on one site. Such savings arise from the two operations sharing common infrastructure elements such as approach roads, hardstanding areas and to an extent buildings, as well as overhead reductions arising from common utilities, services and management costs.

A less obvious way in which recycling and waste disposal can be compatible is in the treatment of mixed refuse which includes organic material. When such waste is landfilled, the anaerobic decomposition and the high moisture content of the waste give rise to both landfill gas and leachate problems as discussed earlier. By composting the waste prior to disposal, these problems can be ameliorated. While it is true that the end product of the composting of such waste would have no value due to the inevitable contamination from other elements of the waste, it would be stable and have a much lower moisture content. Such material could then be used to substitute for alternative materials in use as landfill cover, thereby reducing the amount of landfill void consumed by non-waste materials such as soil. This, then, is an example of how composting can be used as a pre-treatment method for waste prior to disposal to reduce pollution problems arising from landfilling, as well as a means of conserving landfill void space.

Having outlined the various options available for the management of household waste, and considered the compatibility which exists between recycling and other methods of waste treatment, in the next three chapters we examine the mechanics of recycling in detail, starting with the subject of waste collection for recycling.

CHAPTER FIVE

COLLECTION OPTIONS FOR RECYCLING

———————— ◆ ————————

In this and the next two chapters we shall be examining the three basic stages of recycling: collection, processing and reprocessing. While we shall consider these elements individually, it is important to realise that they are inextricably linked and mutually dependent activities as illustrated in Figure 5.1. Clearly, the way in which material is collected directly affects the ability to sort such material and vice versa.

The majority of recent recycling trials have tended to focus primarily on the methods of collection and to a lesser degree on the subsequent processing operations; many have given little consideration to the final reprocessing activities. The design of any recycling scheme should, however, consider these three stages in reverse order. When considering the materials to be recycled, the markets for these materials (the reprocessors) should first be identified and the requirements of these markets, such as the grades and types of material accepted, the forms and levels of contamination tolerated and the volumes and methods of delivery required, should be fully understood. The extent and methods of processing can then be designed in order to produce materials which will meet the markets' specifications and in turn, the methods of collection selected, which will be most appropriate to feed the processing operations.

Clearly, the design of a recycling scheme is not quite as simple as this might suggest, as a number of constraints will also have to be taken into account, such as the existing methods of refuse collection. The consideration of the three stages of

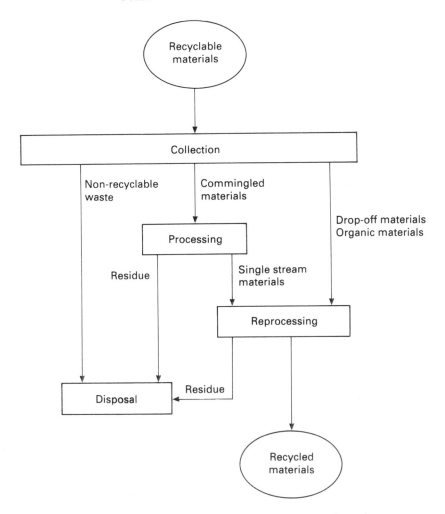

Figure 5.1 The interdependence of the three stages of recycling

recycling may therefore have to be undertaken as an iterative loop, however the emphasis of always considering the requirements of the subsequent stage of the process should never be forgotten.

While the design of a scheme should consider the three stages of recycling in reverse order, it is easier to understand this process if we examine the three individual stages in the order in which they are carried out. We will start therefore with the methods of collection.

Basic collection options

Household waste is collected in three ways, each of which offers scope for the introduction of changes to facilitate recycling:

1) the regular collection from every household of 'dustbin' waste;
2) the collection, at the request of the householder, of large, bulky items such as unwanted furniture or electrical goods; and
3) the delivery by householders of waste to civic amenity sites.

The majority of household waste is collected by the waste collection authority directly from households, usually on a weekly basis, but this can be fortnightly or in some urban areas even twice weekly. A lesser proportion of waste is taken by householders to civic amenity sites and is of a different composition, being primarily garden waste, DIY debris and bulky items.

Let us start then by looking at how the regular collection of waste from households can be changed, in order to facilitate recycling. For the purposes of recycling, the contents of an average dustbin can be divided into three fractions:

1) dry recyclables comprising paper and board, glass, metals, plastics and textiles;
2) organics from both kitchen and garden sources; and
3) non-recyclable residue.

The majority of recycling activity to date has focused on the dry recyclables fraction and two generic approaches have been developed: *bring systems*, which involve householders taking selected materials to designated collection points, and *kerbside systems* which comprise the collection of a range of recyclable materials from individual households followed by the separation of these mixed materials. There are a number of variants or options within each of these two broad approaches and these are discussed in detail below.

Bring systems

Bring or drop-off schemes are the most common form of recycling in the UK at present, primarily because they can be introduced on a small scale, they require minimal capital investment and because they can often be self-funding. The bring system with which the majority of people are most familiar is that of the glass bank, however a wide range of materials including newspapers, cardboard, metal cans, textiles and plastics are today being successfully collected using this approach. Lesser known materials collected by bring systems include oil, domestic batteries and drinks cartons.

The basic principle of a bring system is that the material to be collected is brought by the householder to centralised collection points, where containers are provided for separated materials to be deposited. The form of a bring system is determined by two characteristics: the type of collection container and the density of collection points (measured in terms of containers or sites per head of population).

Figure 5.2 Individual collection containers

Reproduced by kind permission of Rotherham Container Company Ltd

Bring systems originated as individual collection containers, typically a mixed glass bank or a skip type paper bank (see Figure 5.2), located on a site which would allow users to deposit material without having to make a special trip to the site, for example in supermarket car parks or at civic amenity sites. As the range of materials to be collected has increased, these single bank sites have developed into recycling centres (also called neighbourhood recycling centres, community recycling centres or mini recycling centres), typically comprising individual banks for colour separated glass, paper banks and can banks. A typical recycling centre is shown in Figure 5.3.

The trend has been to use smaller and smaller containers to allow sites to be brought closer to the centres of population, in order to increase site density and therefore site usage. The move to smaller containers has also been to overcome a problem with the original large skip type containers, which was that it was extremely difficult to find locations for these containers which were convenient for public access but which also allowed appropriate access to the large collection vehicles which are needed to service such banks.

There is a degree of debate as to whether users of recycling centres visit them on their way to somewhere else, for example whilst shopping, or whether they in fact make a special journey. If recycling centre users do in fact make a special trip to deposit their collected materials, this would clearly have major implications for the siting of such collection points, for example making it less necessary to locate them in supermarket car parks. A second implication, and a far more serious one, would

Figure 5.3 A typical recycling centre

Reproduced by kind permission of Nottingham City Council

be that if such special journeys were being made by car, it is probable that the negative environmental impact of such journeys would far outweigh any environmental benefit of material recycling.

In order to encourage greater use and to reduce the need for special journeys, the latest development in bring systems is that of 'high density' or 'intensive banking', a concept which uses small collection containers, typically 240 litre or 360 litre wheeled bins, grouped together in what are sometimes called micro recycling centres. The materials collected are usually limited to colour segregated glass and metal cans only, at sites in residential or shopping areas. The aim is to ensure that the maximum number of collection points are available to householders, in order to encourage frequent use.

The names used to describe drop-off sites can sometimes be confusing. For example, Westminster City Council calls its sites micro recycling centres but use large, 1100 litre wheeled bins, while Adur District Council has mini recycling centres which use the much smaller 240 litre wheeled bins. However, as site densities have increased in order to make drop-off sites more accessible to users, there has been some evidence of an unexpected householder reaction. While householders would like a site as close as possible for their own convenience, they do not want the site located near to their property (the classic NIMBY 'not in my back yard' syndrome). This is particularly true of glass banks which can give rise to complaints from people living close to them, since the deposit of glass into a bank can often generate a level of noise which is unacceptable, particularly late at night.

Another reason why people do not like drop-off sites to be too close is that unless a site is well maintained, regularly inspected and properly serviced, there can be an accumulation of both litter and material overflow from a bank when it becomes full. For example, if a glass bank is not frequently emptied, the situation can arise whereby a householder takes bottles for deposit and finding the bank full, simply leaves them beside the bank. This generates nuisance from litter and potentially a safety risk from broken glass. In addition many sites, particularly smaller ones, provide containers only for the collection of the required recyclables and not for the deposit of any container used to bring the recyclables to the site, for example plastic bags or boxes. Such containers may then be left by householders at the site, again contributing to the problem of litter.

The experience of many local authorities of operating such sites over the last five to ten years has concluded that:

■   sites must be selected to provide maximum access but minimum nuisance to neighbours;
■   all banks should be frequently emptied to ensure that there is always capacity to deposit delivered material;
■   provision should be made on site for the deposit of non-recyclable material, such as plastic bags or boxes, used to deliver recyclables; and
■   arrangement must be made to maintain sites and in particular to manage the problem of litter.

With regard to this latter point, a number of councils have developed an approach whereby local community or voluntary groups agree to 'adopt a site'. Such a group agrees to monitor and manage their site in accordance with the following guidelines:

1)   to keep the site tidy;
2)   to publicise the facility locally;
3)   to liaise with the local authority or collection contractor on any problems; and
4)   to ensure that collection containers are emptied when required by informing the local authority or collection contractor.

In return they receive all or a share of the proceeds from the sale of the materials collected at the site.

In addition to the NIMBY reaction cited above, a second problem with high density banking is one of simply finding suitable sites. As one would expect, as banks are introduced, those sites which are most likely to give the greatest collected tonnage are selected first and as more sites are needed, less preferred locations must be taken with lower collected tonnages per site.

Bring systems rely on individual householders making the effort to take their recyclable materials to a collection point. Clearly not everyone will be prepared to do this and given the above comments on the problems of siting drop-off containers, there is clearly a limit to the amount of material which can be collected through bring schemes. The absolute value of this limit, which will vary between materials, is a subject for debate, but it is generally accepted that bring systems are unlikely to collect any more than 15 per cent of the total waste stream. So, while bring schemes have formed the foundation of the development of recycling in this country, if we are to achieve high levels of recycling (and specifically the government's recycling target), other methods of collection for recycling will need to be developed. The major alternative to bring schemes is that of kerbside collection.

As will be explained in greater detail below, kerbside collection containers can take the form of bins, boxes or bags. Dry recyclables can be collected in any of these containers, although the collection of glass in bags places the collector at greater risk than with the other methods. Organic material is only collected in bins or bags, but if collected in bags, these must be collected no less frequently than once a week due to problems with infestation and vermin.

Kerbside systems

The two key features which characterise kerbside collection are that:

1) recyclable materials are collected directly from a household rather than the householder being required to take the materials to a drop-off point; and
2) materials are normally collected as a mixture of recyclable materials ('commingled' collection) for example paper, plastics, cans and glass, rather than being segregated into individual materials as with bring schemes.

The choice of materials to be collected and the segregation of the household waste stream by kerbside collection has evolved into three general approaches:

1) **dry recyclables and non-recyclables** – this requires the householder to separate dry recyclables and non-recyclables into either two separate containers or a single divided container (such as a wheeled bin);
2) **organic waste and non-recyclables** – the householder separates organic waste and non-recyclables for kerbside collection, with the option of dry recyclables being collected by an associated bring scheme; or
3) **dry recyclables, organic waste and non-recyclables** – the householder separates two recyclable fractions, dry recyclables and organic waste, requiring the provision of three separate containers.

There are three generic types of kerbside system: Blue Box, Green Bin and Green Bag. In addition, there are numerous variants of the three basic approaches and these are now discussed in detail.

Blue Box

The Blue Box system was developed in North America and has been under trial with a number of local authorities in the UK (notably Sheffield, Milton Keynes and Adur). The term 'Blue Box' has been used in this description to denote the method of collection; in practice, not all of the boxes are blue. For example, in the scheme operated on behalf of Bath City Council, the boxes are green.

Householders place newspapers and magazines, metal cans, glass and certain plastic containers into a 50 litre plastic storage box (Milton Keynes and Adur use two boxes, one for paper, the other for commingled materials). The container(s) is emptied using a special purpose, compartmentalised vehicle into which the materials are sorted at the kerbside. This collection is in addition to the existing weekly refuse collection service. The collection boxes used in Milton Keynes are shown in Figure 5.4 and the original collection vehicle in Figure 5.5.

The Blue Box system, although simple to operate and relatively cheap in terms of container costs, has a number of inherent disadvantages:

- the volume of waste collected is limited by the size of the Blue Box and the range of materials accepted and therefore not all potentially recyclable material is collected;
- dirty tin cans and plastic containers have to be washed before they are put into the box as the box is usually stored within the house;
- Blue Boxes require regular replacement as they lend themselves well to alternative storage uses;
- the maximum recycling rate achieved with a Blue Box kerbside collection would be between 10 and 20 per cent depending upon the operation of the scheme; and
- Blue Box collection has a lower overall household waste collection efficiency due to:

Figure 5.4 Blue Box collection containers

Reproduced by kind permission of Milton Keynes Borough Council

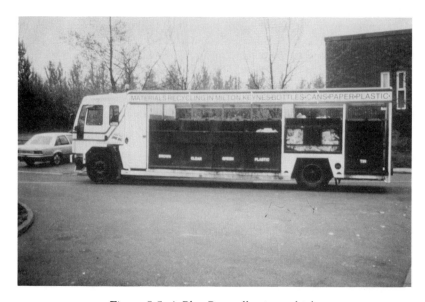

Figure 5.5 A Blue Box collection vehicle

Reproduced by kind permission of Milton Keynes Borough Council

- the need for an additional vehicle and crew to visit each house each week;
- uneven filling of vehicle compartments results in sub-optimal vehicle loading; and
- the handling and sorting of the materials from the Blue Box at the kerbside results in low labour utilisation.

The Blue Box approach does have a significant advantage compared to other kerbside approaches in terms of the quality of the materials collected. Since all material is sorted at the kerbside, unwanted or contaminated material can be rejected at this point, thus minimising the rejection of material during the subsequent processing stage and hence the cost of the processing operation. Direct feedback can also be given to individual householders to improve the quality of the material which is set out for collection.

The collection costs of a Blue Box scheme are high. Many North American municipalities such as Chicago can no longer justify these costs, and are moving away from this approach and are increasingly using the Green Bin or Green Bag systems.

Green Bin

This system uses wheeled bins as the collection container. As with the Blue Box system, the term Green Bin refers to the method of collection rather than the colour of the bins used. There are a number of possible bin combinations which can be used to divide the waste into one, two or three fractions for recycling:

1)   the dry recyclables fraction (typically a green or blue bin);
2)   organic material for composting (typically a brown bin); and
3)   non-recyclable materials (typically a grey bin).

The simplest system uses two bins, one for dry recyclables, the other for non-recyclables (with organic material included in this fraction for disposal). Each bin is emptied on alternate weeks using standard compactor vehicles. The only additional collection cost is therefore the two wheeled bins, one of which may already be in place and which can usually be self-financing, through savings in labour and the provision of refuse sacks. This approach was originally piloted in Bury in Lancashire.

An alternative to the above is to use a single, divided wheeled bin to achieve the same material separation. Such bins are serviced weekly using a compactor vehicle which is itself divided. This approach has the advantages of both reducing the capital funding required (since a divided bin is cheaper than two standard bins) and maintaining a weekly service. In addition, many types of property only have room for a single wheeled bin.

If organic material is to be recovered as a third fraction, a more sophisticated bin combination is required. In Leeds, a pilot trial provides householders with a single bin for dry recyclables and a divided bin (one half for organic waste, the other for non-recyclables). Each bin is serviced on alternate weeks, one by a standard vehicle, the other by a divided vehicle. While this is the most expensive option in terms of capital funding, it delivers the maximum amount of material for recycling.

The original Leeds pilot scheme used two divided wheeled bins as shown in Figure 5.6. The dry recyclables bin (the green bin) included a partition to keep paper and textiles separate from plastics and metals; in later trials this divider was removed. The bins shown are divided front to back. An important lesson from these early trials was that such a division reduced the efficiency of collection, since only one bin at a time could be lifted by the collection vehicle. By dividing the bins from side to side, a twin bin lifting mechanism can be used. A horizontally divided collection vehicle is shown in Figure 5.7.

Green Bag

The collection of commingled dry recyclables in a plastic sack is an alternative development to the Green Bin approach and has the advantage of taking up less storage space, while being likely to be comparable in terms of container cost.

Green Bag schemes are currently under trial in Cardiff and the Royal Borough of Kensington and Chelsea. Reports on these pilot schemes have been favourable with good rates of participation being achieved. The system requires the placing of commingled dry recyclables in the green plastic sack and all other waste in the normal black sack. (In Kensington and Chelsea, recyclables are set out in any plastic bag, such as supermarket carrier bags).

Figure 5.6 Divided wheeled bins

Figure 5.7 A horizontally divided refuse collection vehicle

Reproduced by kind permission of Lacre PDE Ltd

Figure 5.8 Green Bag collection

Reproduced by kind permission of Colin Kirkby, Cardiff City Council

In Cardiff, householders fill their green bags in a particular way (paper at the bottom, then glass and plastic bottles with cans on the top) so as to minimise breakage. The operation of this scheme is shown in Figure 5.8.

The Cardiff pilot scheme operates on the basis of a fortnightly collection of the green bag on the same day as the weekly collection of the black refuse sack but using a separate, non-compaction vehicle. Once delivered to the central sorting plant, the green bags are opened and the contents processed. The bags themselves are included within the recyclable plastic fraction. An alternative collection approach to the Cardiff scheme is the weekly collection of both bags in a divided compactor vehicle as recently implemented in Kensington and Chelsea. Such a vehicle is shown in Figure 5.9.

Combining the collection of recyclables and refuse

One of the disadvantages of the Blue Box system (as operated for example in Milton Keynes) and the Green Bag system (as operated in Cardiff), is that an additional vehicle is used to collect the recyclable materials. If recyclables and refuse can be collected simultaneously but separately within a single vehicle, there are clear financial and environmental savings.

The key to the success of such combined collection is the design of the collection vehicle, an area where development work is continuing. Examples of such new designs have already been referred to and illustrated in Figures 5.7 and 5.9 (horizontally and vertically divided compactor vehicles).

Figure 5.9 A vertically divided refuse collection vehicle

Reproduced by kind permission of Norba Waste Handling Systems Ltd

Figure 5.10 A combined compactor and compartmentalised collection vehicle

Reproduced by kind permission of Worthing Borough Council

A more recent design of vehicle is shown in Figure 5.10. This vehicle, which is on trial in Worthing, combines the REL compactor unit for refuse collection with two side loading compartments for the collection of recyclables (in this case for paper and for mixed plastics and metal cans).

In the Worthing trial, the recyclables are separated by the householders using Blue Box containers (which are in fact green). The collection operators sort the recyclables in these containers into two wheeled bins which are then wheeled to the vehicle and the contents tipped in to the appropriate compartment. When the vehicle discharges each compartment (separately), the paper is simply bulked-up for delivery to market, the mixed plastics and cans are sent to a nearby MRF and the refuse is sent for disposal.

The Worthing trial demonstrates two important principles:

1) that the collection of source separated recyclables and of refuse can be successfully combined, using the most effective technology applicable to the collection of both types of waste; and
2) the processing requirements of recyclables' collection can be minimised by some materials (in this case paper) being sent directly for reprocessing and only the higher value materials being processed in a MRF (in this case plastics and cans).

Clearly, a vehicle such as that on trial in Worthing can only have a limited number of compartments (the practical limit being three or at most four). This means that the degree of kerbside sorting that is possible is limited. There is thus a trade-off between the advantages of combined collection and the advantages of reduced processing which arise from kerbside sorting. Equally, combined collection (or co-collection as it is sometimes termed) can limit the range of materials included in a kerbside scheme (the Worthing example excludes glass).

Which system to use?

Each of the collection methods outlined above has particular characteristics which make it particularly suitable for use in some applications and less suitable in others. A summary of the suitability of each system for collecting specific materials is presented in Table 5.1.

Kerbside systems will in general collect more recyclable materials than bring schemes (with Green Bin or Green Bag collecting more material than Blue Box), but are more expensive to operate simply because they have to collect material from every household rather than from centralised collection points.

If our objective is to achieve recycling at minimum cost, then the preferred method is likely to be a bring system, but it must be accepted that this will only ever achieve a relatively low level of recycling. If, however, our objective is to maximise recycling, the preferred method will be kerbside collection, which will achieve the highest levels of recycling but at a higher cost. A comparison of the general characteristics of the kerbside collection options is given in Table 5.2.

Table 5.1 Summary of collection options

| | Bring | | | Kerbside | |
Material	CA site	Recycling Centre	Blue Box	Green Bin	Green Bag
Paper[1]	(✓)	(✓)	(✓)	✓	(✓)
Plastics[2]	(✓)	(✓)	(✓)	✓	(✓)
Metals	✓	✓	✓	✓	✓
Glass	✓	✓	✓	✓	✓
Textiles[3]	✓	✓	✓	✓	(✓)
Garden waste[4]	✓	X	X	(✓)	X
Food waste[4]	X	X	X	(✓)	X
Wood	✓	X	X	X	X
Oil	✓	X	X	X	X
Building waste	✓	X	X	X	X
Furniture	✓	X	X	X	X
White Goods	✓	X	X	X	X
Batteries[5]	(✓)	(✓)	(✓)	(✓)	(✓)
Hazardous waste[6]	(✓)	X	X	X	X

1 (✓) – only newspapers and magazines; 2 (✓) – only plastic bottles; 3 (✓) – could be included, but no scheme does at present; 4 (✓) – not all Green Bin schemes separate organic material; 5 (✓) – provision for household battery collection could be included; 6 (✓) – separated hazardous waste could be collected, but is not at present

Table 5.2 Summary of kerbside collection options

Characteristic	Blue Box	Green Bin	Green Bag
All potentially recyclable material collected	No	Yes	Potentially
Ease of use	Moderate	Good	Moderate
Efficiency of collection	Poor	Good	Poor/Good[1]
Voluntary or mandatory	Voluntary	Mandatory[2]	Voluntary[3]
Suitable for all housing types	(Yes)	No	Yes
Estimated diversion rate achievable (after processing at MRF)	15–20%	25–40%[4]	20–25%

1 poor if second vehicle used, as in Cardiff; 2 if wheeled bins are to be used, all households must adopt the same system; 3 schemes to date have been voluntary; higher diversion rates could be achieved if the scheme were mandatory; 4 the lower level relates to dry recyclables, the higher level includes organic material collection

At this point it is appropriate to dispel one of the myths of recycling which has arisen through the misuse of the term kerbside. It is often stated that kerbside collection is more suited to urban environments and bring systems to rural communities (the primary difference between the two being the distance travelled by any collection vehicle). This argument is based on the premise that kerbside collection requires a second collection vehicle to visit each household, in addition to the normal refuse collection vehicle, so that the costs associated with servicing sparsely populated rural areas with two vehicles would be prohibitive. However, the only kerbside collection system for which this is true is Blue Box, because with both the Green Bin and the Green Bag systems there is no requirement for a second vehicle, if the scheme is correctly integrated with the normal refuse collection service. Given that every household is already being visited once a week by a refuse collection vehicle, by changing this system to a Green Bin or a Green Bag system, the collection of recyclables can be achieved with no increase in vehicle traffic. A Green Bin or Green Bag kerbside system is thus equally applicable to rural and urban areas. In addition, any bring scheme requires collection vehicles to service the drop-off banks. These vehicles are additional to the normal refuse collection vehicles so that the servicing of banks located in remote locations, such as outlying villages, is a considerable expense. The argument therefore that bring systems are more suited to rural environments and kerbside to urban environments is incorrect. Kerbside collection is equally applicable in both rural and urban areas and since bring systems require the use of additional collection vehicles, the environment in which they are most cost effective is where bank sites are at a high density, in other words in an urban environment.

When planning the introduction of new arrangements to collect recyclable materials, consideration must be given to the different types of housing which exist in the target collection area. The methods of collection must match the needs and constraints of the housing stock. In particular:

- kerbside collection is clearly inappropriate to high rise housing;
- wheeled bin based schemes may be unsuited to terraced housing (particularly two bin schemes); and
- intensive banking may not be appropriate in high density housing areas where space is at a premium.

So far we have concentrated on the collection of household waste. It is, however, a common practice for some commercial waste to be collected with household waste. For example, if a particular household refuse collection round includes a row of shops and the local authority has contracted to collect the commercial waste from these shops, this waste will be collected in the same vehicle as, and together with, the household waste. This clearly has implications for the kerbside collection of recyclables.

Any kerbside collection scheme which includes commercial premises should ensure that premises, such as offices and shops, which dispose of largely uncontaminated recyclable materials, are included within the household collection rounds so that such material can be delivered directly to a central sorting plant. In this case, the commercial premises must segregate their waste into the same fractions as the domestic households. In addition, it will be necessary to agree the proportion of commercial waste collection so that recycling credits may still be claimed for the household materials.

Scheme, support and promotion

The success of any recycling collection scheme depends upon achieving a high level of householder participation and a low level of contamination by soiled recyclables or non-recyclable material. Such success depends upon the provision of clearly communicated, simple instructions, adequate supporting advice and regular feedback on progress.

This is particularly true for the launch of any new collection system, when householders must be told how to use the new system, but just as importantly, be encouraged to use the system. The effective use of both existing local media and targeted communication is essential to both launch and maintain a successful collection system.

Collecting and processing

As stated at the beginning of this chapter, collection and processing are two inextricably linked activities which are mutually dependent, so that the method of collection must be designed to facilitate the subsequent processing operations. When considering these two activities together there is a spectrum of choice as

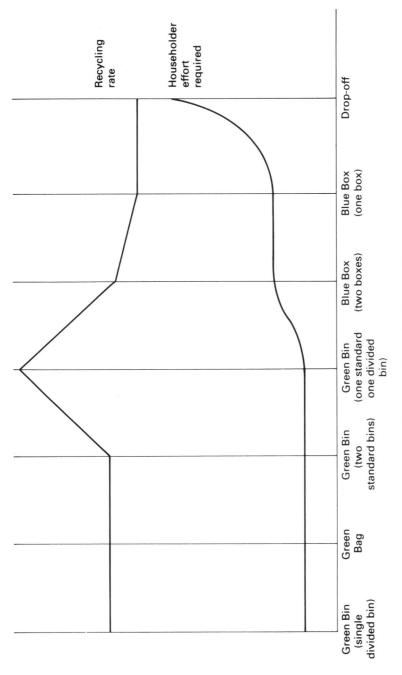

Recycling rate

Householder effort required

Green Bin (single divided bin)

Green Bag

Green Bin (two standard bins)

Green Bin (one standard one divided bin)

Blue Box (two boxes)

Blue Box (one box)

Drop-off

Figure 5.11 The ease of use of different collection methods

illustrated in Figure 5.11, which ranges from the complete source separation of material with no subsequent sorting, typified by bring systems, to the minimum separation at source and the subsequent central sorting of fully commingled recyclables, for example with a Green Bag kerbside system.

Figure 5.11 illustrates one of the key factors to be taken into consideration when designing a collection system, namely the ease with which householders will be able to use that system. For example, while bring systems are less expensive than kerbside systems, they do require much more effort on the part of the householder (one of the reasons why they are less expensive) and therefore will receive a lower level of public support and hence lower collection tonnages. On the other hand, fully commingled kerbside schemes, while being very easy for the householder to use, do involve a greater cost. The trade-off between ease of use and cost is not an easy one and will be influenced by local circumstances.

Figure 5.12 is a flowchart which illustrates and summarises the decision making process that needs to be followed when considering which collection system to select. The diamond boxes represent decision points, the rectangular boxes the consequences of those decisions. This figure highlights one of the decisions which needs to be taken with regard to kerbside collection – whether or not to include glass.

There is an ongoing debate as to whether glass can be collected successfully through kerbside schemes or whether it is better to use bring systems, the method preferred by the glass industry. The inclusion of glass in a kerbside scheme will inevitably result in some glass being broken during vehicle loading and discharge (operational evidence suggests that breakage as a result of compaction in the vehicle is negligible due to the cushioning effect of the surrounding paper and plastic film). Such breakage will reduce the amount of glass ultimately recycled and could give rise to operator safety problems during sorting. The alternative of collecting glass using bring systems is likely to result in much lower collection levels. This is of course no reason why glass cannot be collected via a bring scheme in association with the kerbside collection of the other dry recyclables, as has been done in a number of UK collection trials.

The selection of the appropriate method or methods of collection for recycling is thus a complex process, requiring such diverse factors is to be taken into account as:

- the existing methods of refuse collection;
- the types of housing to be serviced;
- the likely level of public acceptance, and hence use, of any proposed method; and
- the range of materials to be collected.

To this list must be added the evaluation of the costs of collection and the implications for and constraints of the subsequent sorting process. It is this latter issue that we will examine in detail in the next chapter.

COLLECTION OPTIONS FOR RECYCLING

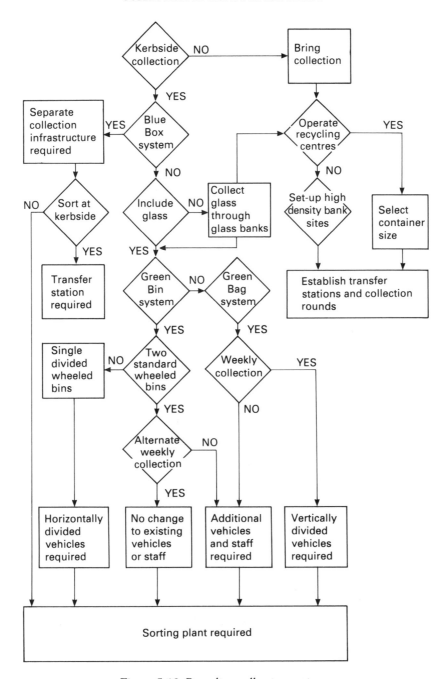

Figure 5.12 Recycling collection options

CHAPTER SIX

THE SEPARATION OF RECYCLABLE MATERIALS

———————— ◆ ————————

In the previous chapter we saw that there are many different ways of collecting commingled recyclable materials. While these methods of collection are clearly different, they all have one thing in common in that, following collection, the mixture of materials needs to be separated. This activity is called 'processing' and is carried out in a central facility. Such facilities have been called by various names such as Sorting Plants or Recycling Plants, but the most commonly used term is the American description of a Materials Recovery Facility or MRF (pronounced 'murph').

We have little direct experience of MRF operation in the UK. A number of small scale pilot MRFs have operated for some time, notably in Cardiff and Leeds and more recently in Sompting in West Sussex. However the first large scale facility only became operational in November 1993 in Milton Keynes. The following description and discussion of MRF design and operation is therefore drawn very much from European and US experience, and interpreted within the UK context.

MRF capacity

MRFs vary in size, which is measured in terms of their throughput capacity. In the USA such sizes range from 25,000 tonnes per annum (tpa) to 200,000 tpa, with the majority being in the range 50–100,000 tpa. The size of a MRF will be determined

62

by a number of factors including the methods of sorting employed, the materials handled and the catchment area the plant is to service. This latter point is a critical factor since it is both financially and environmentally undesirable to transport recyclable materials over long distances in order to process them. High population density areas such as major cities will therefore be more able to support larger sized MRFs, while semi-rural areas will require smaller facilities.

It is likely that in the UK, MRF capacities will be in the range of 25–100,000 tpa. For example the Milton Keynes MRF has a design capacity of 100,000 tpa, but when commissioned was only able to attract 20,000 tpa from the Milton Keynes Borough Council kerbside collection scheme. As a result, the MRF operators are seeking to attract material from neighbouring authorities.

Given that there is a minimum viable size of MRF, any MRF is likely to be serviced by a number of different collection schemes and must be designed accordingly. One specific corollary of this statement is that any MRF should be designed to be able to process recyclable materials derived from both kerbside collection and drop-off sources.

Although the design of any MRF will be optimised to achieve the effective separation of commingled material, pre-sorted recyclables from glass, paper and other banks can also be processed. The benefits of having such a capability include:

- the opportunity to reduce the contamination of drop-off sourced material by MRF processing which will result in a higher end market value based upon improved material purity; and
- the benefit of combining drop-off derived material with sorted commingled material in order to deliver larger volumes to end markets at an improved price for the drop-off material.

The efficient processing of drop-off derived material can be achieved by delivering the pre-sorted material directly to the relevant part of the MRF via by-pass and crossover conveyor belts.

The technical specification of the MRF should also include appropriate flexibility in relation to arrangements for the delivery of recyclables in a variety of containers and vehicles such as:

- divided refuse collection vehicles;
- standard (undivided) collection vehicles;
- bulker vehicles; and
- various drop-off containers or skips.

Material separation

Figure 6.1 illustrates the range of materials which can arise from a commingled waste collection, in the form of a 'materials hierarchy'. The hierarchy identifies the four levels to which the commingled material can be sorted within a MRF, with Level 1 as the simplest degree of separation and Level 4 the most complex.

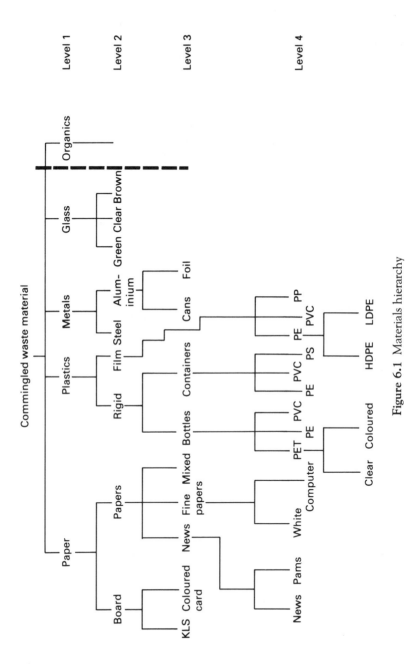

Figure 6.1 Materials hierarchy

Reproduced by kind permission of Coopers & Lybrand

Levels 1 and 2 in the materials hierarchy illustrate the degree of sorting required to separate the basic components of dry commingled recyclable material. These first levels of separation are equivalent to that achieved at a recycling centre where the public are required to place paper, glass and metals into different containers. The separation of dry mixed recyclable material to Level 1 within a MRF is reasonably simple but unlikely to result in an economic return for the effort and investment required.

Level 3 requires a greater effort to sort the commingled material, however the material obtained at this level and at Level 4 allows the supply of material directly into the reprocessing material end markets, thereby bypassing any merchant operations. As the capability of a MRF reaches Levels 3 and 4, the increased cost and effort required to separate commingled material is at least in part offset by the higher financial returns available once the material is sold, as well as the greater availability of end markets into which it can be sold.

The value of sorted material will vary depending upon the level of separation, the degree of contamination and general market conditions. As an example, the value of paper or plastic sorted to Level 1 in 1993 was negligible and may not even have covered the cost of delivery to market. If the same material were sorted to Level 3, newspapers could have been worth £15–20 per tonne and plastic bottles £25 per tonne.

Level 4 characterises the best returns available for sorted material. This level differs from Level 3 in that the separation is based upon material type, such as PET or PVC as opposed to material use, for example bottles, containers or cans. The value of material sorted to Level 4 is significantly higher than Level 3. In 1993, mixed plastic bottles attracted a price of £25 per tonne whereas plastics separated into material type (PET, PVC and HDPE) were worth £75–£100 per tonne.

While the main objective in establishing a MRF is to achieve a high degree of commingled material separation as efficiently as possible, it is not essential that all material types identified at Level 1 are sorted down to a uniform level within the hierarchy. Sorting different materials to varying levels within the hierarchy will result in a characteristic *materials profile* for the facility. This materials profile can be developed either to meet the specific recycling objectives of the facility or based upon purely financial grounds and will in turn be dependent upon the materials targeted for collection. The materials profile will also clearly reflect the local markets for separated materials, for example, there may be greater benefit in sorting plastics to Level 4 than in the case of paper.

The extent to which a MRF is capable of achieving an appropriate Materials Profile at commercially acceptable operating costs will be directly linked to the selection of appropriate levels of manual and automated sorting technologies. The three basic approaches to the use of manual and/or automated technology for the separation of materials may be summarised as follows:

1)   manual sorting;
2)   combined manual and automated sorting; and
3)   automated sorting.

Each of these approaches is examined in detail in the following sections.

Manual separation

The simplest approach to material separation uses people to hand sort the commingled materials. Operators remove defined categories of material from a conveyor belt which carries the mixed materials past a series of picking stations. Selected materials are dropped into bins beside the picker or thrown across the conveyor belt into collection chutes. For some materials this is the only sorting option, for example paper grading or the colour separation of glass (although automation to colour separate whole glass bottles is being developed, notably in the Netherlands). Individual plastic polymers can be successfully hand sorted using a combination of recognition rules which include the nature of the product itself, for example all carbonated drinks bottles are manufactured from PET. Metal items are less suitable for hand sorting, for example steel and aluminium drink cans cannot be separated manually as the products are visually identical.

Manual separation has the advantages of being able to achieve a high degree of separation and a high quality of separation with a relatively low capital investment, but has the disadvantages of any labour intensive process, that is, high labour costs and potential performance variation due to fatigue. In addition, there are growing concerns regarding the health and safety aspects of manual sorting, in terms of airborne dust inhalation, risk of injury from sharp objects such as broken glass and injury through repetitive movements. These concerns can, however, be addressed successfully using localised environmental controls such as air circulation and filtering, protective clothing such as Kevlar gloves, job rotation and ergonomic design. An example of the manual separation of paper, board and plastic film is illustrated in Figure 6.2 and a photograph of a manual MRF is shown in Figure 6.3.

The effective separation of commingled material relies upon the skill of trained operators to achieve the high level of quality required by the material end markets.

The effectiveness and efficiency of the manual sorters can be considerably improved by the inclusion of specific features such as the following:

- 'Head on sorting' whereby the operator separates three material categories from a conveyor moving towards the picking station. This is achieved, for example, by the operator selecting brown and clear glass into storage bays either side of the belt and allowing the third and largest volume fraction (ie green glass) to fall off the end of the conveyor into another bay and/or conveyor.
- 'Negative sorting' which requires the operator to select those materials which form the smaller proportion of the stream thereby allowing the larger volume fraction to fall unaided into a dedicated storage bay. An example would be the negative sorting of magazines from a paper line whilst newsprint continued to the end of the conveyor.
- The appropriate education of householders who are responsible for the initial separation at source to assist the MRF sorting efficiency by:
  - removing the tops from plastic bottles or securing tops and puncturing the container (to allow compaction during baling);

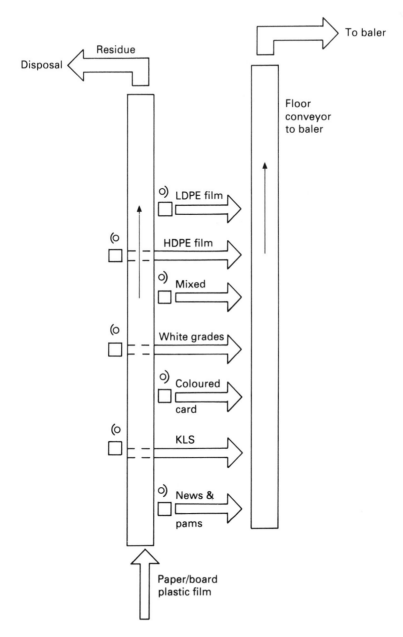

Figure 6.2 Manual paper, board and plastic film separation

Reproduced by kind permission of Coopers & Lybrand

Figure 6.3 A manual sorting operation

Reproduced by kind permission of Triselec (France)

- crushing tin cans in order to avoid other materials becoming trapped inside;
- minimising contamination by rinsing containers; and
- ensuring that different recyclable materials are fully separated.

Manual/automated separation

The operating performance of the predominantly manual MRF described above can be significantly enhanced by the appropriate addition of specific automated MRF technologies. Such an approach results in the following benefits:

- improved material sorting efficiencies;
- lower unit sorting costs;
- enhanced operator safety; and
- access to wider markets for some materials, for example plastics, which can be sorted, washed and processed to achieve higher levels of quality.

There are a number of approaches which use localised automation to replace elements of the hand sorting of materials. A schematic illustration of a MRF using limited automation to enhance the manual sorting process is shown in Figure 6.4 and is described below, and an example is shown in Figure 6.5.

Commingled recyclable materials comprising any combination of paper, glass, metals and plastics, are transferred from the tipping floor (a) to a rotating trommel

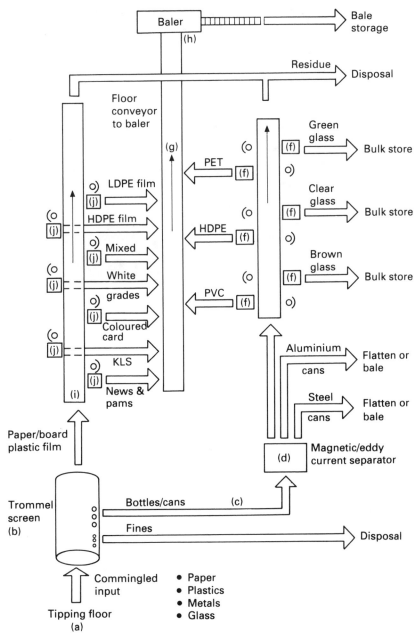

Figure 6.4 Commingled sorting plant (limited automation)

Reproduced by kind permission of Coopers & Lybrand

Figure 6.5 A partly automated MRF

Reproduced by kind permission of Milton Keynes Borough Council

screen (b) via a rising conveyor belt. The trommel creates three streams of material:

1) fines;
2) containers (for example, glass and plastic bottles and metal cans); and
3) bulky items such as paper, cardboard and plastic film.

Small non-recyclable materials and fines are collected for disposal and the bottles and metal containers transferred via conveyor (c) to the magnetic separator (d). The combination of automated electro-magnetic and eddy current separation technologies at (d) allows an efficient three-way sort. This is illustrated in Figure 6.6 and is carried out as follows:

1) Ferrous metals are held onto the conveyor as it runs back below the head pulley to a point where the magnetic attraction ceases. The cans then fall into a dedicated hopper.
2) Aluminium is ejected from the end of the conveyor to a hopper positioned slightly past the end of the belt.
3) Plastic and glass containers fall off the end of the conveyor into a third hopper which feeds the sorting line.

A photograph of such a separation unit in operation is shown in Figure 6.7.

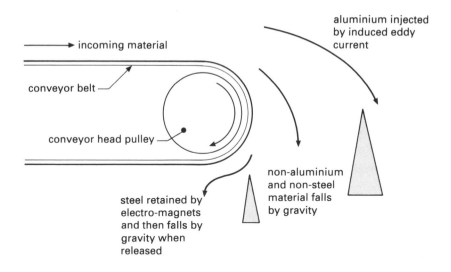

Figure 6.6 Magnetic and eddy current separation

Figure 6.7 Magnetic and eddy current separation

Reproduced by kind permission of Milton Keynes Borough Council

This three-way separation, while being an efficient process, may require final manual sorting or checking of the separated materials depending on the mix of incoming materials. In the case of aluminium, other materials such as plastic bottles may be knocked into the wrong hopper by the ejected metal, and if both aluminium cans and foil are included in the collection scheme, these will have to be separated by hand, due to their being made from different aluminium alloys.

The steel and aluminium cans are fed from their respective hoppers by conveyor either for mechanical flattening prior to being blown by compressed air directly into a waiting vehicle container, or are fed to dedicated balers. The aluminium foil is, if included, negatively sorted from the aluminium conveyor and stored for baling.

The plastic and glass bottles are transferred to the sorting line (e), which operates on the basis of manual operators selecting the three different colours of glass and three basic types of plastic bottle from the remaining mix of materials.

The sorting line (e) is elevated above ground level and the operators place segregated bottles into individual storage bays (f) located below the work stations. The storage bays hold the segregated materials until appropriate volumes have been accumulated, prior to being transferred directly to transport vehicles in the case of glass and the baler (h) in the case of plastic bottles.

The baler (h) is linked to the segregated material storage bays by a floor conveyor (g) which runs parallel to the sorting lines. The baler is capable of compacting different categories of segregated material into standard sized bales; however, the density and weight of the bales will vary. The baler is operated on a batch basis with segregated materials being sent for baling only once a volume threshold has been reached. Materials are transported from the storage bays to the baler conveyor by a front end shovel loader, or by the floors of the storage bays themselves being conveyors.

Completed bales are transferred via fork lift truck to dedicated storage areas. Once a full lorry load has been collected, arrangements will be made to transfer separated materials to the end markets.

Paper products and plastic film fall out of the trommel (b) onto a conveyor leading to sorting line (i). This second sorting line consists of a series of picking stations for operators to remove the required categories of paper and plastic films. The number of picking stations in use at any one time will vary with the types of material required for end markets and the input stream.

The segregated materials obtained from sorting line (i) are also dropped into dedicated storage bays (j) from where they are transferred to the baler conveyor (g). Any unsorted residues run into storage containers located at the end of the two sorting lines, from there they are delivered to a collection point for disposal.

Such a sorting plant can accept commingled recyclable material from either household or commercial sources. It has the flexibility to accept both commingled and relatively pure input steams, for example material comprising largely office waste paper from a commercial source would bypass the trommel and be transferred directly to sorting line (i) for the separation of paper and plastic film. The operational flexibility enables high value commercial wastes to be sorted and baled efficiently on a batch basis. Such a capability will enable the MRF operator to maximise income potential from material sales and therefore reduce overall operating costs.

The efficiency of hand sorting of commingled materials can be greatly improved if the range and types of materials in the mix is reduced. This can be achieved using automated techniques based on size separation (that is, screening) or based on separation by weight (for example, air classification). In this way light, bulky items such as paper and board or plastic film can be separated from smaller, heavier items such as bottles and cans. Alternatively lighter objects can be separated from heavier objects of the same size, for example plastic bottles from glass bottles. Streaming materials in this way reduces the range of materials to be selected by hand, making the selection task simpler for the human picker.

This concept of streaming can be extended to include the material collection system. In particular, by separating the bulky items such as paper, board and plastic film from the container fraction (plastic and glass containers and metal cans) at source, the design of the MRF can be simplified and its separation performance improved. If such a source separation can be achieved, referring to Figure 6.4, the need for the trommel screen is eliminated and the two streams of material are fed directly to conveyor (i) and to the magnetic separator (d). Such stream separation at source is likely to achieve a higher degree of separation than a trommel screen and will therefore improve the subsequent material sorting.

Two stream separation at source is common with Blue Box collection schemes and since this is the predominant method of collection in North America, the majority of US and Canadian MRFs operate on this basis. Indeed, the Milton Keynes MRF uses this system. Such a source separation is less easy and more expensive to achieve for Green Bin and Green Bag systems, but can be achieved as follows:

- **Green Bin** – a two bin combination with the recyclables bin being divided to keep paper, board and plastic film separate from recyclable containers; or
- **Green Bag** – the provision of an additional, but different coloured bag for bulky materials (these two recyclables bags could be co-collected in the same collection vehicle and then colour sorted after delivery to the MRF, such sorting being by hand or using automation which has recently been introduced into the UK from Denmark).

Clearly the streaming of materials at source will increase the complexity and cost of collection, but will reduce the complexity and cost of sorting. Striking the balance between the complexity of collection and sorting requires careful consideration and will depend very much on the methods of collection and the materials being collected and can be a major influence on the overall cost of recycling.

Automated separation

Fully automated systems for the separation of commingled materials have been in existence for many years. These systems use a combination of screening and classification techniques which utilise the physical properties of the materials, such as size, weight and surface area, to achieve the desired separation. However, such separation techniques cannot achieve the same degree or quality of separation as that of hand sorting. Such plants therefore produce lower quality, mixed grade materials which attract lower market prices than an equivalent manual plant. Clearly an automated sorting plant will have a significantly higher capital cost and significantly lower labour costs than an equivalent manual plant.

The extent to which a MRF is automated will be dependent upon a number of factors such as:

- the material input characteristics;
- the material output requirements;
- the material throughput;
- the capital and revenue costs/funding; and
- the need for flexibility.

The manual approach to sorting allows considerable flexibility in response to changes in both the materials delivered to the facility and end market demands. Such a manual MRF has the advantage of being able to accept a wider range of material types than an automated version. The material can also be separated into a broader range of outputs. This type of facility is characterised by low initial capital expenditure on equipment but high operating costs due to high staffing levels.

In contrast, once designed and installed, an automated MRF will be constrained in terms of the range of material accepted, as well as sorted material outputs. This reduced level of flexibility is due to the unadaptable nature of the processing equipment used, although it is likely to provide a higher level of material throughput than is possible with a manual MRF. Use of this option will result in higher initial capital expenditure but lower operating costs due to fewer staff being required.

Bottle sorting
Figure 6.8 highlights the bottle sorting line (f) shown in Figure 6.4. Automated techniques exist for the separation of glass and plastic bottles which utilise the difference in weight between the two materials.

One such technology involves the glass and plastic moving over an inclined sorting machine where gravity/density principles coupled with traversing metal chain curtains automatically separate the lighter, bulky plastic bottles from glass. The glass is heavy enough to pass through the steel curtain to the lower side of the inclined conveyor while the plastic is retained at the top. The two fractions fall into separate hoppers for further sorting operations. Glass bottles and jars can be passed through up to three such inclined curtains before reaching the main glass line for hand separation by colour. A high level of operator safety is achieved by small pieces of broken glass being removed via an intermediate vibrating screen.

Figure 6.9 illustrates an automated system for the separation of plastic bottles into individual polymer streams. One such system utilises a sensor (k) to identify the chloride ions contained within PVC materials which are subsequently ejected

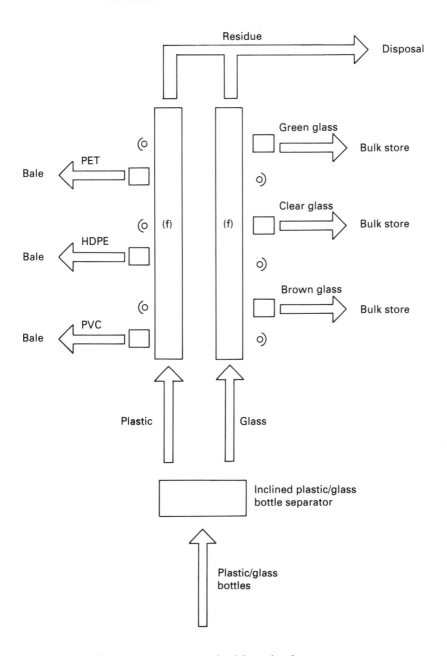

Figure 6.8 Automatic glass/plastic bottle separation

Reproduced by kind permission of Coopers & Lybrand

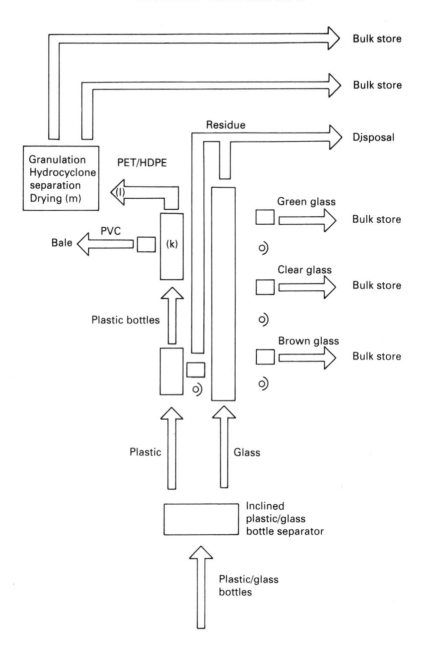

Figure 6.9 Automatic plastic bottle separation

Reproduced by kind permission of Coopers & Lybrand

from the conveyor by compressed air. The remaining plastic bottles consist of PET and LDPE. These containers are passed through a granulator (l) after which the plastic flakes are separated by density via hydrocyclone separation (m) (this process is described in detail in Chapter 7). The efficient automatic separation of mixed plastic polymers is however not yet fully developed. Investment in this type of automated sorting technology is expensive, but the added value in terms of increasing the number of available end markets as well as value of the separated material may result in a commercial return.

Any MRF should by designed to allow manual sorting operations to be replaced by proven automated techniques as they are developed, however it must be emphasised that even if such technologies are adopted, a minimal level of manual involvement will still be required to ensure the required level of quality is achieved and maintained.

Transport of separated materials to end markets

The transport of separated materials will be a significant operating cost especially if end markets are some distance from the MRF.

There is a cost benefit to be gained from flattening steel and aluminium cans and transporting them loose (ie unbaled) to end markets. Although the process results in a less dense level of compaction in the container, the simplified processing is more cost effective. Furthermore, glass bottles and jars can be crushed prior to delivery in order to achieve a higher level of compaction thereby improving transport efficiencies.

The current limits of MRF technology

Figure 6.10 illustrates a MRF design incorporating as much automation as is currently practical. Commingled input material is conveyed from the tipping floor infeed pit up to a bag splitter (n) (if required) after which it passes a pre-sort platform for the removal of bulky items. The mixed waste stream then passes through the rotating trommel screen to produce three separate streams of material segregated by size:

1) small size fines for disposal;
2) medium sized containers (glass bottles and jars, plastic bottles and containers and metal can and foil containers); and
3) bulky items (paper, plastic film, and board products such as boxes).

The container stream is sorted in a series of sequential steps:

1) magnetic extraction of steel cans;
2) eddy current separation of aluminium cans and possibly foil, followed by the manual separation of these two grades;

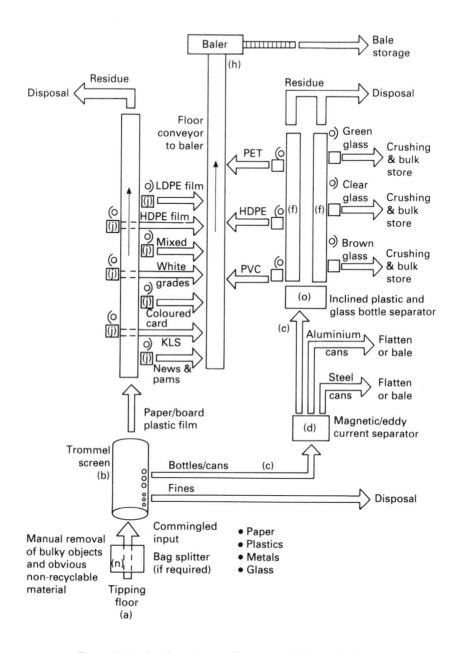

Figure 6.10 Combined manual/automated MRF technology

Reproduced by kind permission of Coopers & Lybrand

3) glass and plastic containers separated automatically by the use of an inclined sorting table (o);
4) manual removal and colour sorting of glass either via a linear sorting line or three-way head on sorting; and
5) manual sorting of plastic containers into three individual polymer types and where appropriate, colour grades.

The bulky items stream is manually separated utilising a linear sorting line or a head-on sorting cascade as appropriate, to separate the following grades (groups refer to the UK standard groups of waste paper):

■ **Paper:**

  – one or more pulp substitute white grades (groups 1–3);
  – news and pams (group 5);
  – old KLS/container (group 8);
  – mixed papers (group 9); and
  – coloured card (group 10);

■ **Plastic:**

  – HDPE film; and
  – LDPE film.

The MRF concept shown in Figure 6.10 illustrates how automation can be used to improve the sorting of materials, but also shows that some degree of manual separation will continue to be needed, either because the use of automation is inappropriate or because the quality requirements of the reprocessing stages can only be met by manual sorting.

What is also clear is that the point at which processing ends and reprocessing begins is not necessarily fixed, a good example of this being the recycling of plastics. We examine reprocessing in the next chapter.

CHAPTER SEVEN

HOW RECYCLABLE MATERIALS ARE REPROCESSED

——————— ◆ ———————

Having examined the collection and processing of recyclable materials, we will now consider the third stage of recycling, that of material reprocessing. The key characteristic of this stage is that the form of the recyclable material is changed. In the first two stages of recycling such material is merely handled, but in this final stage there is a physical change in the form of the material to produce a recycled material. Thus, paper is repulped, glass and metals are remelted and plastics are granulated and may be re-extruded. In all cases the materials are cleaned and contraries removed.

We will now look in detail at the reprocessing of the following recyclable materials:

■ paper
■ glass
■ aluminium cans
■ steel cans
■ plastics
■ textiles
■ organic material.

Paper

Paper reprocessing, as with paper production from virgin fibre, comprises two stages: stock preparation and paper making. However, the preparation of stock from waste paper is more involved than with virgin pulp, due to the contraries and mixture of papers involved.

Stock preparation

Stock preparation can include a number of different stages, depending on the waste paper being reprocessed and the grade and intended application of the recycled product.

Preparation starts with pulping, in which the paper fibres are separated by agitation in water. The ratio of fibre to water is described as the consistency, with a low consistency being six per cent and a high consistency 15–18 per cent. After pulping the stock needs to be cleaned to remove contraries. The degree and methods of cleaning employed need to strike a balance between rejecting good fibres and failing to remove unwanted contaminants. Again, the grade and intended application of the recycled product will determine the degree of residual contamination acceptable. The initial cleaning of the pulp has traditionally been by the use of a 'ragger rope' which hangs in the rotating pulp and large contaminants, such as plastic film, become entangled with the rope and are removed.

The most serious contaminant problem is that caused by what are called 'stickies'. These are adhesive materials, for example the strips of adhesive used on self-seal envelopes, which if not removed or treated can lead to significant reductions in paper machine productivity or product quality. Stickies can be removed at a number of stages in the stock preparation process and the current trend is to operate the process so as to keep the stickies as large as possible to maximise their removal.

After pulping the stock is screened to remove contaminants, using coarse screening to remove large contaminants and fine screening to remove finer material. Another method is centrifugal screening which uses hydrocyclone technology to separate contaminants using differences in density. Thus materials heavier than fibre and water can be separated, such as metal or grit, as can lighter materials such as plastic or wax.

Depending on the grade of waste paper and its intended use after reprocessing, the stock may also require de-inking following screening. This is the process of removing printing inks from the fibres and can be achieved by washing or flotation. With washing, the stock is sequentially diluted and thickened, with the particles of ink being removed as the water is removed, literally washing the fibres. Flotation is a process whereby air is bubbled through the stock, which is pretreated with what are called 'collector' chemicals which coat the ink particles and make them water-repellant. The hydrophobic particles then adhere to the air bubbles and are carried to the surface where they form a froth which can be readily removed. Washing requires the ink particles to be small, typically less than 15 micron, whereas the flotation process is able to remove larger sizes of ink particle. One of the problems of de-inking is the variety of printing inks and processes in use and the variation in the size of ink particle produced on pulping. In order to cope with this situation combinations of washing and flotation de-inking are often used.

Depending upon the end use application of the recycled paper, bleaching may be required to improve the brightness of the finished paper. The lack of brightness may be caused by the presence of lignin in the waste paper feedstock or by the inclusion of contaminants. Lignin is the naturally occurring polymer which binds the fibres together in wood and which is present in mechanically pulped paper. Lignin contributes to the yellowing of such papers which occurs under the action of ultraviolet light or heat. The bleaching or brightening process chemically modifies the lignin, but differs from the bleaching of virgin paper as the process is one of colour removal, rather than actual lignin removal, so that lower concentrations of bleaching agents (such as hydrogen peroxide, chlorine or oxygen) are needed.

A final stage in the stock preparation process may be that of dispersion, a chemical treatment of residual contaminants to reduce their size to one which allows their inclusion in the finished paper (if less than 40 microns in size they will not be visible to the human eye).

Paper making

Once the stock has been prepared, the consistency is diluted to approximately one per cent (to prevent fibres flocculating, or clinging better) and any required fillers or chemicals added. The suspension is then sprayed onto a fast moving fabric belt, on which water is removed first by gravity and then by vacuum suction, to increase the consistency to about 20 per cent. The paper web is then passed through pressure rollers to remove more water, resulting in a consistency of approximately 50 per cent, that is half fibre, half water. The majority of the remaining water is then removed by evaporation as the paper is passed over a series of steam heated rollers. At the end of the paper machine, the finished paper is wound onto a reel for onward handling.

Glass

Virtually all glass which is collected is source separated by colour, since the three colours of clear (or white), green and brown (or amber) are reprocessed separately.

After delivery to the reprocessing plant, the recyclable glass (called *cullet*) passes under an electromagnet which removes ferrous contaminants and through a manual sorting operation, where contraries such as plastic or aluminium bottle tops and non-glass items are removed. The cullet is then crushed to a uniform size, passed under a second electromagnet and sieved. The cullet then receives a final inspection prior to passing into bulk storage. Up to 80 per cent cullet can be used in a glass making furnace.

Aluminium cans

Aluminium used beverage cans (UBCs) can be recycled in much the same way as any aluminium scrap, however the greatest demand for aluminium UBCs is for reprocessing to produce new can feedstock. In this way, the particular alloy required for can manufacture is retained within a closed loop, giving significant technical and financial advantages.

There is only one plant in the UK which converts aluminium UBCs back into can feedstock and that is the BA Alloys facility in Warrington which opened in November 1991. The 50,000 tonne per annum plant, when operating at full capacity, is able to reprocess 25–30,000 tonnes of UBCs each year (the balance is scrap from the can making process), which represents approximately one-third of the total UK aluminium can annual consumption.

The reprocessing cycle operates as follows. UBCs are delivered to the plant as bales or briquettes and following weighing and inspection, the bales are broken open and mixed with scrap from new can manufacture. The material is then shredded to less than 75mm in size and evenly distributed on the carrying conveyor for feeding into the electromagnetic separator (to remove ferrous material, such as steel UBCs). Approximately 2 per cent of the incoming material is ferrous. The material is then passed through the decoater, in which all paint and lacquer is removed under the action of 280°C gas burners. The cleaned material is transported to the melting furnaces where melt samples are taken, and any adjustments to the alloy composition are made. The main addition is magnesium, with some silicone also being added. The furnaces operate at a temperature of approximately 800°C.

From the melting furnaces, the molten aluminium is passed to the tilt furnace, where it is held prior to casting. The metal is degassed in the tilt furnace and large oxide particles removed. When ready for casting, the tilt furnace is slowly tilted and the molten alloy channelled to the casting mould via two further filters. The alloy is cast into 27 tonne ingots, in what is effectively a continuous casting process. Each ingot is nine metres in length and is equivalent to approximately 1.5 million aluminium cans. After casting and cooling, the ingot is sawn to size and despatched for rolling into sheet.

The production of an aluminium ingot is the end of the recycling process. What has been produced is an ingot which is identical to that produced from virgin material and which is used in the production of new aluminium cans.

Steel cans

Steel cans can be collected in a number of ways and the methods of collection determine the subsequent method of reprocessing.

Steel cans have a thin surface coating of tin to prevent the oxidation (rusting) of the steel body of the can. If the cans are collected by magnetic extraction from the residue of an incinerator, this tin coating will have been removed by the heat of the incineration process. Such cans are then reprocessed in the same way as any steel scrap, by remelting, casting and rolling.

If, however, the cans are collected in such a way as to leave the tin plate layer intact, for example by bring collection or by magnetic extraction at a MRF or *prior* to incineration, the reprocessing operation must remove this tin plate layer. Such a process has been developed by AMG Resources Limited, who operate two steel can reprocessing plants in the UK, one in Llanelli and one in Hartlepool.

The AMG process recovers both the steel and the tin content of the cans. Cans are received in loose, flattened form, or as bales (a maximum bale density is set, to ensure that the cans can be separated prior to processing). The cans are passed through a trommel screen to remove large contaminants and are then shredded in a patented device called the Cutler Shredder. The shredder comprises a contra-rotating cage and impeller. As the cans are fed into the shredder (individually but at high speed) they are impelled towards one another. The cans therefore undergo a series of high speed collisions which result in the cans shredding one another and all labels, paint or lacquer and any product residue in the cans (such as food) being stripped from the resulting fragments.

After shredding, the material is passed under electromagnets which extract the steel fragments in the form of dense, tin plate pellets from any unwanted residue. Aluminium is also then extracted (from bimetallic cans such as steel drinks cans with aluminium ring-pull ends) from the residue, either by air classification or by eddy current separation. AMG report that 98 per cent of unwanted residue is removed in this process and 99 per cent of the aluminium content.[36]

Once the steel fragments have been separated they must be de-tinned to recover both the steel and the tin. The de-tinning is carried out using an electrolytic process, in which the tinplate forms the anode in an electrolytic cell. The electrolyte is a solution of caustic soda at 70–90°C. As an electric current is passed through the cell, the tin is plated out onto steel cathodes, from which it is subsequently mechanically stripped, leaving the steel fragments free of tin. In this way, both the steel and tin are recovered for general use by the respective metal industries, and in addition, any aluminium from bimetallic cans is also recovered.

The AMG plants in Hartlepool and Llanelli have capacities of 15,000 and 20,000 tonnes of used cans per annum respectively. This represents a combined capacity of approximately 875 million cans per annum.

Plastics

Recyclable plastics are classed either as *rigid*, for example plastic bottles, or *films* such as carrier bags or biscuit wrappers. The basic stages of reprocessing are similar for both forms of plastics, but the two are processed separately. There are also key differences in the way that different polymers are treated. The main steps in the reprocessing of any plastic are as follows.

Recyclable material is received in baled form and after weighing and inspection, the bales are broken open. The loose material is then visually inspected and any contraries manually removed. The material is then granulated (chopped or shredded into small pieces called *flake* or *regrind* and of the order of 25mm^2) and washed to remove all non-plastic contaminants. Following washing, the wet flake is passed through one or more separation processes, depending on the particular polymer being reprocessed, to separate out any unwanted polymers. The resulting single polymer stream is then dried using both mechanical and thermal methods (such as pressing to remove water and hot air drying).

Depending on the polymer being reprocessed, the drying stage will either be followed by bagging of the flake for sale or this final stage will be preceded by the dried flake being recompounded. Recompounding comprises the mixing of additives with the flake, or blending with other reprocessed material or virgin polymer, followed by extrusion to produce a finished pellet form (called *regranulate*), which is then bagged for sale. An alternative to recompounding is the pulverisation of the flake (*micronisation*) to produce a powder which is then bagged for sale.

Three of the above stages – washing, separation and recompounding – are discussed in more detail below. We then consider the specific processing of plastic bottles in more detail, followed by the processing of mixed plastics.

Washing

Following granulation, the plastic flake is washed to remove all non-polymer material. The principal contaminating materials are paper from labels (and associated adhesives), residue from the previous contents of the container and general dirt and debris accumulated either during the containers' use or during the post-use collection, processing or handling. The degree of non-polymer contamination can be significant, for example, used agricultural film can comprise 50 per cent non-polymer by weight and the contents residue of plastic bottles can account for as much as 20 per cent of the apparent bottle weight.

The primary method of washing is called 'friction washing' and uses aggressive mechanical agitation of the plastic flake in water to separate the contaminating material from the flake. This is how paper labels are removed. The process may be augmented by using hot water and/or the addition of chemicals such as detergents. However, many reprocessing plants simply use a cold water friction wash to clean the material.

Separation

Once the flake has been washed, any unwanted polymers must be separated out. Different polymers have different densities, so that when suspended in water, some will float and others will sink. For example PET has a specific density of 1.34 tonne/m^3 and that of polyethylene (PE) is 0.9 tonne/m^3, so that in water, which has a specific density of 1 tonne/m^3, the PE will float and the PET will sink, allowing a mixture of the two polymers to be separated. Table 7.1 gives the specific densities of the polymers most commonly found in household waste.

There are two basic separation techniques in common usage: sink-float tanks and hydrocyclones. The former is a simple device in which a mixture of two polymers suspended as flake in water, flows into a settling tank. The heavier polymer sinks in the tank and is drawn off from the base of the tank; the lighter material floats on the surface of the water, from where it is drawn off. A hydrocyclone is a more sophisticated device in which the waterborne mixture of polymers is rapidly rotated. Again, the heavier material sinks and the lighter fraction floats; however the geometry of a hydrocyclone can be designed so that the apparent specific

Table 7.1 Polymer specific densities

Polymer	Specific density (tonnes/m³)
PVC	1.35–1.39
PET	1.34
Polystyrene	1.09
Polyethelene	0.9

density of the carrying liquid (normally water) can be changed, so that a range of pairs of polymers can be separated using the same carrying liquid. For example, PET and HDPE can be separated in water since PET is heavier and HDPE lighter than water. However, polystyrene has a specific density very close to that of water. By changing the apparent specific density of the water in a hydrocyclone, so that it is between that of HDPE and PS, the two polymers can be separated.

This ability to design a hydrocyclone to achieve the separation of different pairs of polymers can be used to progressively remove unwanted polymers from a mixture of more than two. For example, a bale of PET bottles will inevitably contain polyethylene and polypropylene (from bottle tops) and may contain PVC and polystyrene from incorrectly sorted containers (many PET bottle tops also contain PVC seals). In processing much material, a series of hydrocyclones may be used to sequentially separate out the polyethylene and polypropylene, the PVC and the polystyrene.

Recompounding

Once any unwanted polymers have been separated from the primary polymer and the resulting high purity flake has been dried, this recycled material can either be bagged and sold in flake form or processed further, depending on the polymer and its intended use. Any additional processing takes the form of recompounding. Recompounding is a process in which additives are mixed with the recycled flake, for example to alter its colour or to add ultraviolet light stabilisers, and/or the recycled flake is blended with other recycled flake or virgin polymer, for example to change the melt index of the resulting polymer blend. After mixing and blending, the polymer is passed through an extruder which further blends the material prior to heating the polymer above its melting point and feeding it under pressure through a filter (called *melt-filtration*) to produce a final pellet form (called *regranulate*) for bagging and sale.

Plastic bottles

Plastic bottles are manufactured from one of three polymers: high density polyethylene (HDPE), PET or PVC. In addition to the bottles themselves, the bottle tops can be made from HDPE, polypropylene or aluminium.

Technology has been developed to automatically identify different polymers in order to facilitate automated bottle sorting. However, the only polymer for which sensing is currently available is PVC. Such sensors use X-rays to detect the presence of chloride ions in the PVC. Sorting is achieved by passing a stream of mixed bottles under the sensor, and when a PVC bottle is detected it is automatically ejected from the bottle stream. Such a device can thus be used to positively sort PVC bottles, either to produce a PVC stream from a mixed bottle stream, or to remove stray PVC bottles from a pre-sorted HDPE or PET stream. This method of separation is particularly important in PET reprocessing since the similar specific densities of PET and PVC effectively preclude their separation in a hydrocyclone. Sensors which use infra-red detection techniques are being developed which could be capable of identifying not only each polymer, but also bottle colours.

In theory, a mixed stream of PET, HDPE and PVC bottles could be automatically sorted, first by detection and separation of the PVC bottles, followed by hydrocyclone separation of the PET and HDPE flake. In fact, this was the basis of the Reprise DSR 2000 concept which was piloted during the early 1990s. However, the trials demonstrated that the necessary quality of polymer separation cannot be achieved using such technology. Both PVC sensing and hydrocyclone separation can be used successfully to remove low levels of unwanted polymer, from a near single polymer stream, but the required high degree of separation of mixed polymer bottles can only be achieved effectively through the manual sorting of bottles. The reprocessing of plastic bottles has therefore moved from a starting point of processing mixed polymer bales to one where the bottles are pre-sorted (either by the householder or at a MRF) prior to delivery to the reprocessing plant. The reprocessing of each of the three bottle polymers is described briefly below.

HDPE reprocessing

The majority of plastic bottles are manufactured from HDPE. Typical applications are for household products, for example washing liquids or other cleaning products and cosmetic or hygienic products such as creams, soaps or shampoos. Other products such as emulsion paints and motor oil are also sold in HDPE bottles. Colours range from the natural opaque milk jug to white, black or any other colour. Experience has shown, however, that the colour that results from reprocessing post-use household HDPE containers is remarkably consistent both in colour, a light blue (provided any black containers are excluded) and in the melt index (being more consistent than virgin polymer).

The reprocessing of HDPE, following grinding and washing, requires a series of separation stages to remove all polymers except polypropylene (which as a similar polyolefin, cannot be removed by hydrocyclone technology, and the presence of which has no detrimental effect on the performance of the recycled HDPE) followed by drying and recompounding.

The yield of recycled HDPE, from a pre-sorted input stream is of the order of 70 per cent (6–7 per cent loss due to labels, 1 per cent in melt filtration and the remainder due to product residues in the bottles), with less than 0.2 per cent non-polymer contamination.

PET reprocessing

PET bottles must be reprocessed to a very high level of purity, typically to include less than 50 parts per million of impurities. The majority of recycled PET is spun into fibre for use as a filling material, for example in padded clothing such as anoraks or in bedding such as sleeping bags or quilts, or woven to produce industrial strapping similar in appearance to car seatbelts. The spinning process requires a very high quality of feedstock, hence the demanding standard required of PET bottle reprocessing. This is also an example of the reprocessed material being reused in a high value application, hence the ability of the reprocessor to offer the higher price for PET than for other polymers.

The most common use of PET bottles is the bottling of carbonated drinks. The majority of such bottles are clear, but there are a number of green, amber and brown bottles also in use. Coloured bottles are hand sorted prior to granulation and either rejected or processed as separate batches. The carbonated drink PET bottle is easily identified as it has either a coloured base cap (normally made from HDPE) or the distinctive 'petal' shaped base.

Clear PET bottles are also used for non-carbonated liquid containment, and care must be taken when sorting, for example in a MRF, not to confuse these with clear PVC bottles. As indicated earlier, PET and PVC cannot be separated in a hydrocyclone, so that all PVC must be removed from a PET bottle stream, either by use of a PVC sensor (for whole bottle removal) or by hand. A particular problem is the PVC seals used in some PET bottle tops (for sealing carbonated drinks). A PVC sensor cannot be used to detect this material, so to ensure that all such PVC is removed, all PET bottle tops must be removed by hand prior to bottle grinding. If the tops have not been removed prior to the bottles being collected, this must be carried out in the reprocessing plant and is a very expensive operation.

Following granulation and washing, the PET stream is passed through a hydrocyclone to remove any remaining polyolefins, prior to drying and sale as flake.

PVC reprocessing

PVC bottles are used in non-pressurised applications which require a clear or tinted material. Typical uses are for cooking oil, cosmetics and non-carbonated mineral water. Following separation, the PVC bottles (including the polyethylene and polypropylene tops) are granulated and washed prior to hydrocyclone separation to remove the residual polyethylene and polypropylene. Following drying the flake is pulverised to produce a fine powder, since this is the form in which the majority of virgin polymer is produced.

Mixed plastics

Mixed plastics can be reprocessed to produce a material, often described as a wood substitute, which is increasingly used in open air applications such as fencing and street furniture. The structure of the reprocessed material is essentially a matrix of polyethylene with small particles of other polymers and contaminants, such as paper or metal, suspended within this matrix.

Mixed plastics are first granulated and then the light fraction (predominantly polyethylene film) is separated from the heavier fraction by air classification. The two fractions are then recombined in the required ratio to ensure a polyethylene rich mixture. This is then extruded to form finished profiles with a grained texture, which form the basis of the material's subsequent use (for example, round or square sections for fence posts etc).

All non-polymer contamination, including for example food waste from plastic film, remains in the blended mixture. The heat and pressure of the extrusion process are relied upon to both sterilise and stabilise any such degradable contamination.

The normal colour of such material is black, but colour master batches can be added prior to extrusion to produce in particular brown material (to enhance the wooden appearance).

Textiles

Textiles are delivered in loose form either from textile bank collections or from charity shop donations to the reprocessing mill. The reprocessing is essentially a manual sorting operation, to produce three streams of material to be used as:

1) second-hand clothing for export to less developed countries;
2) industrial wiping cloths; and
3) filling materials.

Clothing is sorted by garment type and quality so that, for example, trousers, skirts and dresses which are of suitable quality for reuse are segregated and baled for shipment overseas. All other textiles are sorted into man-made and natural fibres, and depending on the end use, may be sorted by colour.

Such sorting can only be carried out manually and requires considerable skill since textiles can be sorted into over 100 different grades. The grades required are dependent upon short-term market requirements so that flexibility in the sorting operation is essential.

Organic material processing

The organic elements of the household waste stream broadly comprise the following:

- kitchen waste;
- garden waste; and
- industrially processed organic material such as paper and leather.

Kitchen waste is predominantly food waste, including vegetable matter, animal products such as meat or bones and processed foods such as cheese. All such material may be raw or cooked. Garden waste is almost exclusively vegetable matter which is either woody or soft in nature.

The two methods of organic material processing are *composting* and *anaerobic digestion*. Each of these methods is discussed individually below, and a brief comparison of the two methods is then presented.

Composting

Composting is a natural process of decomposition which occurs in the presence of oxygen, indeed a ready supply of oxygen is essential to the process. Bacteria and other micro-organisms break the organic material down into carbon dioxide, water and the compost residue. The process also requires the presence of water and is exothermic, that is, it generates heat. The process of composting is thus very much one of correctly controlling these three key elements of oxygen, water and heat.

Composting has three basic stages: preparation, decomposition and maturation.

1) **Preparation:** can take a number of forms. Large contraries need to be removed, but generally screening to remove smaller contraries such as plastic or glass is not carried out until after maturation, since too much organic material would be lost at the preparation stage. Large woody items such as hedge, shrub or tree prunings are shredded to reduce them in size and incoming material may be mixed or blended to adjust both the structure and the carbon:nitrogen (C:N) ratio of the incoming material. Typically the structure of the material requires approximately 20 per cent woody material, in order to provide adequate ventilation and the C:N ratio will be about 20:1 for household waste.

2) **Decomposition:** Following preparation, the decomposition stage can be carried out in a number of ways. The material can be handled in *windrows* or enclosed bays, can be covered or uncovered and aeration can be by mechanical turning or by forced airflow.

    The simplest system is that of open air windrow composting. The material is laid out on a hard surface such as concrete, in rows approximately two metres high and three metres wide at the base. A small percentage of previously composted material may be used to seed the process, or as a surface cover to reduce odours. The material is mechanically turned on a regular basis, either by a machine which proceeds along the windrow, taking material in at the front, agitating it and depositing it at the rear of the machine or by equipment which picks up the material of an existing windrow and deposits it to one side, thus creating a new, parallel windrow. The primary purpose of the turning is to aerate the pile in order to introduce the all-important oxygen and thus to prevent the decomposition becoming anaerobic, but it is also used as a method of temperature control and to ensure that all of the material is treated, not just that at the core of the windrow. There is, however, a clear balance to be struck between introducing oxygen and maintaining the pile's temperature.

    The natural triangular shape of the windrow and the need to provide space for mechanical access between windrows means that windrow composting requires a large surface area. The alternative of bay composting follows similar principles, except that the material is contained in rigid bays, which change the triangular section of the windrow to a rectangular one, and which eliminates the need for access between the rows of material since the equipment for turning the material is supported by the bay walls. Such a system is clearly less land intensive, but does require a physical structure to be built.

Aeration of the material can be by mechanical turning as described above, or by the forced passing of air through the material, without turning. This second method is called 'static pile aeration' and can be based either on pumping or sucking air into the pile. Vacuum induced ventilation has the advantage that any odours are drawn back into the pile and can if necessary be treated. The more common method of blowing air into the pile has the advantage of conveying the heat from the most rapidly decomposing waste at the centre of the pile to the outer, cooler regions.

Both the temperature and moisture content of the material must be regularly monitored during the decomposition. If the temperature becomes too low, the decomposition will slow and any pests, seeds (in particular weed seeds) and pathogenic bacteria (such as salmonella) will not be killed off, and if too high, the mesophilic micro-organisms (those not tolerant to heat) will be killed off. If the moisture content falls, the microbial activity slows down; if the moisture content is too high, the air spaces in the material structure can fill with water and the process become anaerobic.

The completion of the decomposition process is not easy to define, and various methods are used including the reduction in the C:N ratio and/or heat generation as the microbial activity decreases. For known materials and composting conditions, the process can simply be controlled on the basis of elapsed time.

In terms of environmental impact and public nuisance, care must be taken during the decomposition stage to control:

- leachate from the pile;
- pests and vermin; and
- odour.

Much of the water content of the material is given off as water vapour during decomposition, although some leachate can be generated. Composting areas should therefore be bunded for leachate collection and appropriate arrangements made for its reuse or disposal. The pests involved are most notably flies and not rodents (as often feared by objectors to composting), since the material is warm and thus unattractive to animals. Odour can be a problem, particularly if the process goes anaerobic. Covering the pile with previously composted material can minimise both fly and odour problems, as can operating in a fully enclosed environment. As a result of the potential problems of pests and odour, unenclosed composting sites are usually remote from centres of population.

3) **Maturation:** When the decomposition phase is complete, the material must be matured in order to allow the decomposition process to be completed. Some of the products of the decomposition stage can be harmful to plant life, so a final slow decomposition is allowed to take place to convert these to harmless products.

Following maturation the compost is screened to remove contraries and may be further screened by particle size to produce different end products, for example the selection of particle sizes less than 10mm for use as a soil conditioner and greater than 10mm for use as a mulch.

Anaerobic digestion

Anaerobic digestion (AD) is primarily a method of energy recovery rather than material recovery. As a method of material reprocessing it is thus outside the scope of this book, however a brief description of the process has been included for reference purposes and to highlight the differences between AD and composting.

AD is a process involving the decomposition of organic material in the absence of oxygen. The process produces carbon dioxide and methane (together referred to as *biogas*) and a residue (called *digestate*). The process is carried out in an enclosed vessel (the reactor) and the biogas collected for use as a fuel. The digestate is either aerobically composted or applied directly to land (the best known example of this being sewage sludge).

The development of AD in the UK is in its early stages with only a small number of pilot projects being undertaken.

Comparison of composting with anaerobic digestion

A comparison of the key features of composting and anaerobic digestion is presented in Table 7.2.

Table 7.2 Comparison of composting and anaerobic digestion

Feature	Composting	Anaerobic digestion
Outputs	Heat, carbon dioxide, water vapour, compost residue	Methane, carbon dioxide, process water, digestate residue
Airborne emissions	Ammonia (odour)	Hydrogen sulphide (odour)
Feedstock	Solid	Slurry
Sanitisation of residue	Yes	No
Volume reduction	30–40 per cent	Low reduction
Capital costs	Low if not enclosed	High
Extent of UK experience	Medium	Low

Adapted from Bardos[37]

CHAPTER EIGHT

THE MARKETS FOR RECYCLABLE MATERIALS

———————◆———————

When we talk about the markets for recyclable materials, we need to be very clear what we mean. There are two different, but related markets:

1) the markets for *recyclable* materials
2) the markets for *recycled* materials.

This is illustrated in Figure 8.1.

The markets for recyclable materials are the reprocessing industries (glass manufacturers, paper mills, metal smelters etc). Recyclable materials are purchased by these industries as raw materials, against defined technical specifications.

Reprocessors convert the recyclable material either into a recycled product which can be sold directly to the consumer, or into a secondary raw material which is used by product manufacturers to produce the final recycled product.

When talking about the markets, the majority of people are referring to the reprocessing industries; however, the requirements of the markets for recycled materials must always be considered, since without this market the recycling loop cannot be closed.

In terms of the markets for recycled materials, there is a further subdivision:

■ where the recyclable material is converted back into a form which is similar or identical to virgin material; and

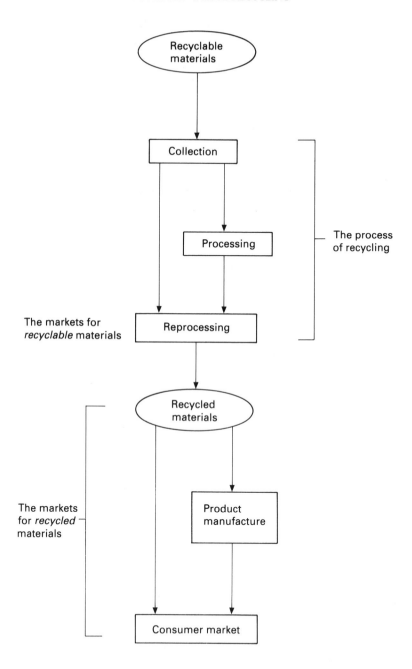

Figure 8.1 The markets for recyclable and recycled materials

■ where the recyclable material is converted into a product which differs significantly from that for which the recyclable material was originally used.

Examples of the first category are old glass containers being made into new glass containers, used aluminium beverage cans being recycled into new cans, or waste paper being converted into recycled paper. With regard to the second category, the recycling of used plastic containers and film into wood substitute products, rubber tyres into carpet underlay or road surfacing materials, discarded clothing into mattress fillings or waste paper into automotive interior components, are all examples of the recyclable material being converted into a product which differs from the material's original form.

At present, the markets for recyclable materials in the UK are, in the main, the reprocessing industries who are serving the first category of market for the recycled materials. So, for example, the strongest markets are for glass, paper and metal reprocessing where the material is simply converted back into its original form. The second category of recycled material market is developing only slowly, as it becomes increasingly clear that our capacity to reprocess material into its original form is unlikely to be able to develop sufficiently to absorb all of the recyclable material potentially available. In many instances, this form of reprocessing would be technically or economically undesirable.

The following analysis of the markets therefore begins with a review of the current markets for recyclable materials and then goes on to discuss how these and new markets can and need to be developed.

Current markets

The existing markets for recyclable materials may be divided into three categories in terms of market demand:

1) **strong demand:** metal cans, glass and textiles;
2) **capacity limited demand:** paper and potentially green glass; and
3) **emerging demand:** plastics and compost.

This is reflected in Table 8.1 which presents a summary of the current levels of post-consumer recycling and which shows higher rates for cans, glass and paper, with the future expansion of paper recycling being clearly limited by current production capacity. This table also shows the current very low level of post-consumer plastics recycling.

The existing markets for glass, paper, cans and plastics are discussed in more detail below.

Glass

Glass was one of the first materials to be collected from post-consumer sources for recycling. Glass which is collected for remelting to produce new glass is known as

Table 8.1 Current markets (1993)

Material	Collection ('000 tonnes)	Production ('000 tonnes)	Consumption ('000 tonnes)	Recycling rate (% consumption)	(% production)
Paper & board	3317	5363	10,254	32.4	61.8
Glass	361	1714[1]	1810	19.9	21.1
Plastics[2]	3	4700[3]	2000[4]	0.2	
Steel cans	102.1	–	641.8	15.9	–
Aluminium cans	19.6	–	93.9	20.9	–

1 Consumption based on waste arisings; 2 British Plastics Federation (1991); 3 All plastics production; 4 Estimate of amount of plastics arising in municipal solid waste

cullet. The use of cullet in new glass production can reduce the energy requirement of this process by approximately 25 per cent (equivalent to 30 gallons of oil for every tonne of cullet used), which is why glass is an economically attractive material for recycling. This is reflected in the relatively high prices offered for collected glass, typically £20–25 per tonne.

Table 8.2 gives a summary of the glass composition in household waste.[35] Ninety-eight per cent of this material is container glass (bottles, jars etc) with the remainder being items such as light bulbs and flat (window) glass. It is the container glass which the glass industry recycles.

For many people, their first (and sometimes their only) experience of recycling has been their use of a local bottle bank. The collection of glass through bring systems is well established in this country, albeit at a low level, and this is the glass industry's preferred method of collection.

However, the name 'bottle bank' has itself lead to a degree of misunderstanding amongst the public in terms of what glass can be recycled. This is illustrated by Tables 8.3 and 8.4 which show that while clear glass represents nearly 60 per cent of the glass that we throw away, less than 35 per cent of all collected glass is clear, representing a recycling rate of only 11 per cent of apparent consumption. Conversely, green glass comprises only 26 per cent of our discarded glass, yet it makes up over half of all glass collections and achieves a recycling rate of nearly 42 per cent of apparent consumption.

Table 8.2 Household waste – glass composition

Container			% weight of total waste stream
Glass	:	clear	5.37
	:	green	2.39
	:	brown	1.31
Other glass			0.20
TOTAL			9.27

Table 8.3 Comparison of glass availability and recycling

Type	% in household waste stream	% collected for recycling
Clear	59.2	33.1
Green	26.4	51.4[1]
Brown	14.4	11.5
TOTAL	100.0	100.0

1 Includes mixed colour collection

Source: British Glass and adapted from Table 8.2.

Table 8.4 Glass recycling by colour 1993

Type	Collection ('000 tonnes)	Consumption ('000 tonnes)[2]	Recycling rate (% consumption)
Clear	120	1072	11.2
Green[1]	200	478	41.8
Brown	41	260	15.8
TOTAL	361	1810	19.9

1 Includes mixed colour collection
2 Based on 20m tpa household waste and percentages shown in Table 8.2

Source: British Glass Manufacturers Confederation and adapted from Table 8.2

This inconsistency is as a result of the general public not understanding that all glass containers may be put into bottle banks, not just bottles. This misunderstanding results in a large proportion of clear glass in the form of jars and food bottles (for example jam jars and sauce bottles), not being taken to bottle banks for collection. In order to address this problem, some glass collectors now refer to the collection containers as 'glass banks', but the name 'bottle bank' appears to have become too well established and much more effort is needed to re-educate the public.

With regard to green glass recycling, there is a foreseeable limit to the demand for this material from current sources. This is illustrated by Table 8.5 which shows that over 70 per cent of new green glass containers are already produced from cullet. The UK does not manufacture large quantities of green glass containers (approximately 17 per cent of all glass container production), but we do import very large quantities in the form of wine and beer bottles. There is thus a considerable imbalance between our consumption and our capacity to recycle green glass, which is going to limit the market for this material in the not too distant future. This problem is exacerbated by the fact that all mixed colour cullet can only be recycled into green glass, hence the recent move by the glass industry to discourage mixed colour cullet collection.

Table 8.5 Glass recycling 1993

Type	Collection ('000 tonnes)	Production ('000 tonnes)	Recycling rate (% production)
Clear	120	1,168	10.3
Green	183	287	70.0[1]
Brown	41	259	15.8
Mixed	18		
TOTAL	361	1,714	21.1

Mixed cullet assumed to be recovered in green fraction

Source: British Glass Manufacturers Confederation

The glass industry has committed itself to achieving a target of recycling 50 per cent of all glass by the year 2000.

Paper

The wide variety of types of waste paper are grouped into eleven grades as shown in Table 8.6, with these grades being further grouped as follows:

- pulp substitute grades : grades 1–4, used for the production of printing and writing papers and tissue products;
- de-inking grades : grades 3–5, used primarily in the production of newsprint and tissue products; and
- bulk grades : grades 6–11, used in the production of board and packaging.

The majority of waste paper from household sources falls into the second and third categories, with the largest element, approximately 49 per cent, being newspapers and magazines (group 5). The remainder are bulk grades in terms of Kraft Lined

Table 8.6 UK standard groups of waste paper

Group	Description
1	white woodfree unprinted
2	white woodfree printed
3	white and lightly printed mechanical
4	coloured woodfree
5	heavily printed mechanical
6	coloured kraft and manila
7	new kraft lined strawboard
8	container waste
9	mixed papers
10	coloured card
11	contaminated grades

Strawboard (KLS) or corrugated cardboard, coloured card such as cereal packets (group 10) and mixed paper (group 9). While household waste does contain pulp substitute grades, for example white letter quality paper from junk mail and other correspondence, the proportion of such grades is very low and it is questionable as to whether it is economical to collect these grades, in which case they will be included in the mixed paper grade.

Table 8.7 presents data on waste paper usage in 1993 and shows that the recycling rate varies significantly by new paper product and in terms of production and consumption. The average recycling rates of 62 per cent of production and 32 per cent of consumption reflect the fact that we produce only 52 per cent of the paper that we consume.

The data in Table 8.7 would suggest that for the majority of new paper products, we are currently using as much waste paper as is possible in terms of UK production, with the exception of graphic papers and to a lesser extent packaging papers. If the recycling rate for graphics papers were increased to the current average of 62 per cent of production, this would create an additional demand of approximately 870,000 tonnes per annum and would increase the recycling rates to 78 per cent of production and 41 per cent of consumption. However, such a change would be dependent upon both technical issues and consumer acceptance of such products, an issue which is addressed later in this chapter. However, in terms of significantly increasing the amount of wastepaper used within current production capacity, graphics papers would appear to offer the greatest scope.

It is also clear from Table 8.7 that if we are to significantly increase the current recycling rate of 32 per cent of consumption, this could only be achieved if additional production capacity were installed to reduce new paper product imports; newsprint is perhaps the best example of this.

The supply of and demand for waste paper has historically been cyclical in nature. When demand was strong, attractive prices were offered, stimulating increased collection. If demand fell or increased collection led to over-supply, prices fell and collection activity consequently reduced. This situation has now

Table 8.7 Waste paper recycling 1993

New paper product	Production ('000 tonnes)	Consumption ('000 tonnes)	Wastepaper usage ('000 tonnes)	Recycling rate (% production)	(% consumption)
Newsprint	741	1932	542	73	28
Graphic papers	1636	3527	146	9	4
Case materials	1369	2204	1467	107	67
Packaging papers	101	405	45	45	11
Packaging boards	688	1205	529	77	44
Tissue	540	681	420	78	62
Other packaging and board	290	299	168	58	56
TOTAL	5364	10,254	3317	62	32

Source: Paper and Pulp Information Centre

changed. In the late 1980s the success of household waste paper collection in North America generated a surplus of de-inking grades which, when traded on the world market, pushed prices to low levels. Prices have been further reduced in Europe by the collection in Germany and exporting of very large quantities of de-inking and bulk grades through the Duales System Deutschland (DSD). This depression of waste paper prices to an all-time low is expected to become the norm, throwing the waste paper merchant sector into crisis.

The market demand for waste paper will only increase if new reprocessing capacity is developed. The expansion in early 1993 of Stirling Fibres plant at Ramsbottom from 50,000 to 80,000 tonnes per annum for tissue product production, was a rare occurrence. The only other expansion of capacity at present is the expansion of SCA's newsprint mill at Aylesford in Kent, which will generate a demand for 465,000 tpa for de-inking grade materials.

To put this in perspective, if all of the de-inking grades discarded annually in household refuse, which are not currently recycled, were to be recycled (approximately 4.3 million tonnes), additional capacity equivalent to nine times the planned capacity for Aylesford would be required.

Cans

Metal cans are either tin-plated steel or aluminium, with a minority of drinks cans being a combination of these, that is a steel body with an aluminium ring-pull top. All food cans are steel while drinks cans (empty drinks cans are referred to in the trade as used beverage cans or UBCs) are either steel or aluminium in the ratio of 40:60.

Aluminium UBCs
Almost all aluminium cans collected for recycling are processed at the British Alcan foundry in Warrington (the remainder being used in general aluminium smelting operations) which takes aluminium UBCs and reprocesses them into aluminium ingots to be used in the production of new cans (a truly closed loop system).

In 1989 the Aluminium Can Recycling Association (ACRA) was established to develop aluminium can collection. In 1992, ACRA announced the establishment of six regional centres which would accept UBCs on behalf of the Warrington plant and pay the same gate fee as available at Warrington. This move was to overcome the problem of suppliers of UBCs who were a long way from Warrington, incurring very high transport costs in order to deliver the material and so being less inclined to do so.

Table 8.8 shows that the current recycling rate of almost 21 per cent is well below the capacity of the Warrington plant, so that the market demand for aluminium UBCs in the UK is currently unlimited.

Steel cans
Steel can recycling in 1993 achieved a recycling rate of 15.9 per cent as shown in Table 8.8. Of the 102,000 tonnes collected, 88 per cent was by magnetic extraction

Table 8.8 Aluminium and steel can recycling 1993

| | Consumption | | Collection | | |
	billion cans	'000 tonnes	billion cans	'000 tonnes	Recycling rate (% consumption)
Aluminium	5.56	93.9	1.16	19.6	20.9
Steel	11.0	641.8	1.75	102.1	15.9

Source: Aluminium Can Recycling Association
Steel Can Recycling Information Bureau

of cans (either from mixed refuse at refuse transfer stations or from ash at incinerators), 5 per cent was via Save-a-Can bank collections and 7 per cent was by other collection schemes such as kerbside collection. An industrial electromagnet can separate out up to 80 per cent of the steel in mixed refuse and the economics of the operation make it attractive to local authorities who operate large refuse transfer stations or incinerators.

Cans which are magnetically extracted from incinerator ash are added directly to the steel making process, since the tin plating is removed during the incineration process. Steel cans from other sources may either follow this route or be detinned in order to recover the tin as a separate metal. The only company offering such a service is AMG Resources Ltd who operate plants in Llanelli and Hartlepool. The combined capacity of these plants is 35,000 tonnes per annum which is less than 5 per cent of current steel can arisings. The cost of transporting steel cans to either of the two AMG plants, compared with the price offered for such cans (between £20–25 per tonne) often makes it uneconomical to send them for detinning, so that many cans are sold directly to local steel scrap merchants.

In July 1993 the 1000th Save-a-Can bank was installed (200 local authorities take part on the scheme). The steel industry has set a target of recycling 50 per cent of all steel cans consumed by the year 2000, indicating that there will be continued demand for new collection schemes for the foreseeable future.

Plastics
The markets for post-consumer plastics are as yet very limited, but can be said to be emerging. There are three factors which have so far limited the development of these markets:

1) the perceived difficulty of separating the high number of plastics used, into individual polymers;
2) the requirement for such used plastics to be washed as part of the reprocessing operations; and
3) the cost of reprocessing compared with the price of virgin plastic.

While in excess of 20 different plastic polymers are used in the manufacture of consumer goods, the primary interest in terms of recycling is in plastics packaging, the majority of which is produced from only six polymers, as shown in Table 8.9.[38]

Table 8.9 Plastics packaging composition

Polymer	Rigid '000 tonnes	%	Film '000 tonnes	%
Polyethylene	686	67	219	89
Polypropylene	63	11	80	8
Polystyrene		8	115	
PVC	15	8	96	2
Polyester	3	4	55	
Other	8	2	17	1
TOTAL	775	100	582	100

As may be seen from this table, the production of plastics packaging is dominated by polyethylene, both for film applications (such as carrier bags and other wrappings) and for rigid containers (such as bottles and boxes).

There are therefore far fewer polymers to separate than many people imagine and the methods of polymer recognition to enable separation are well established. The main barrier to the development of post-consumer plastics recycling is one of cost. The cost of reprocessing such material is high compared with the cost of virgin material, in particular because post-use plastic has to be washed as part of the reprocessing operation.

The reprocessing of *post-industrial* plastic waste is, in contrast, well established and economically viable, since such material is normally single polymer and is clean, so that reprocessing is a straightforward operation. Post-consumer plastics are however, contaminated through contact with the product which they have been used to package and through contact with other materials during collection. This contamination must first be washed out, which is expensive and there are very few companies in the UK who have invested in such washing equipment, hence the market demand is small.

A second limiting factor which exacerbates the high cost of plastics reprocessing is the fact that plastics are very light materials. The cost of transporting plastics for reprocessing is thus very high (plastics must be baled in order to achieve anything like a reasonable payload on a delivery vehicle) and if the material must be transported a long way, in order to deliver it to one of the few plants capable of processing such material, the associated transport costs can be prohibitive.

If post-consumer plastics recycling is to be developed as an economically viable activity, the reprocessing plants required need to be situated as close to the source of supply as possible. This is a very good example of an emerging market, where the suppliers of recyclable material (the collectors) and the markets for the material (the reprocessors) need to work closely together, to match supply and demand, in volume and quality terms and in terms of physical geography.

Recycled plastics can be used either to replace virgin polymers or can be reprocessed as mixed plastics to produce wood-substitute materials. In terms of virgin polymer substitution, the markets for recycled plastics are only limited by the fact that such material cannot be used for applications where it would be in direct contact with food, and some products and/or production processes might have to be slightly modified in order to be able to accept recycled plastics. Plastic wood substitute materials are growing in their usage but have a major difficulty in that they are competing with a relatively low cost and aesthetically pleasing alternative. With both virgin and replacement wood substitute markets the problem facing recycled plastics is their limited ability to compete on price.

The apparent lack of markets

Many people believe that the current low level of household waste recycling in the UK is caused by the lack of available markets for recyclable materials. This absence of stable markets, paying high prices for recyclable materials, is the reason most often cited for there being such a low level of recycling. While it is true that there are limits to our capacity to reprocess some of the recyclable materials in the household waste stream, the perceived lack of markets is not in fact the main reason why the level of recycling is currently so low. The main barrier to increasing today's level of recycling is in reality the widespread availability of cheap landfill. Disposal of waste by recycling currently costs more than disposal via landfill and while this situation prevails, recycling will not develop.

In recognising that recycling costs more than landfilling, many people involved in the collection of materials for recycling (in the main, local authorities and voluntary groups) attempt to fund the additional costs of recycling by seeking high prices for the recyclable materials that are collected. The fact that the required high prices are not being offered by the various reprocessing industries concerned (the markets) is then cited as the reason why recycling cannot develop; but to expect industry to pay high prices for low value waste materials is unrealistic.

If recycling is to develop to a significant level we need to redefine what we mean by a market for recyclable waste. A market should be seen only as the destination for collected recyclable waste, where reprocessing of that waste material will take place. Markets should only be expected to guarantee to accept and carry out the reprocessing of waste; they cannot be expected to fund the costs of recycling. We therefore need to separate the concept of markets (as reprocessors of recyclable material) from the economics of recycling and address them as two separate issues.

Identifying and creating stable markets

To many people, stability in a market refers to the prices offered for the recyclable material that is to be reprocessed. Hence, for example, the market for waste paper has been seen as unstable as market prices fluctuated. However, taking our revised definition of a market as being simply that of a reprocessor of recyclable material, a stable market should be seen as one which is able to accept a given quantity of recyclable material on a regular and consistent basis. Stability is thus simply an issue of demand for materials.

The corollary of seeking a stable source of demand is that collectors of recyclable materials must be in a position to offer stable supplies of material for reprocessing. To meet a stable demand, collectors must be able to provide supplies which are stable in terms of volume, quality and frequency of delivery. This requires planned, controlled and effective methods of collection to be employed. In particular, with regard to the quality of the materials collected, the methods of collection must be matched to the requirements of the market. It is a basic tenet of recycling that you should not collect material for which you have no market. This applies not only to types of materials but equally and often more importantly, to the quality of the collected materials.

There are markets in the UK where the current capacity to reprocess is exceeded by the quantities of material that would be available, if all of the available recyclable material were to be collected. Two obvious examples are the market for low grade waste paper such as newsprint and the market for green glass. There is thus a need to expand the demand for such materials. However, there are two reasons why existing reprocessing capacity will be slow to expand.

1) **Lack of consumer demand** for the products of reprocessing (the markets for recycled materials). Taking the case of low grade waste paper, one of the end products of reprocessing is newsprint. The present relatively low level of recycled fibre content in newsprint, approximately 30 per cent, means that the demand for secondary fibre and therefore the reprocessing capacity to produce this fibre is limited. Until consumers demand a higher percentage of recycled fibre in their newspapers, there is no incentive for the reprocessing industry to expand its current capacity. In order to encourage the use of recycled fibre in newsprint, in 1991 the government reached a voluntary agreement with the Newspaper Publishers Association, the Newspaper Society and the British Newsprint Manufacturers Association, by which the industry will seek to achieve a 40 per cent recycled fibre content by the year 2000.

   Taking the second example of green glass, in the UK we consume more green glass containers than we manufacture (as a result of the high levels of, in particular, wine imports). Unless alternative uses are found for this material (other than producing green bottles) or until consumers accept products other than wine in green glass bottles, the reprocessing capacity for this material will remain at current levels.

   The capacity to reprocess recyclable materials is clearly dependent upon the demand from the markets for recycled materials. Thus if we wish to develop stable markets for recyclable materials, we must first address the issue of how to stimulate this consumer demand.

2) **Lack of stable supplies of recyclable material**. This is something of a chicken and egg situation, in that collectors will not collect materials while there is little or no market demand and the markets will not invest in new reprocessing capacity unless there is a guaranteed supply of materials for reprocessing. A good example of this is post-consumer plastic waste. Apart from a very

limited number of reprocessors with the necessary washing plant to deal with post-consumer plastic waste, there is no volume market for this material. The question is thus one of who will take the risk and act first, the collector or the reprocessor?

Technical and economic advantages and disadvantages of recycled materials

When compared with virgin materials, recycled material is often considered to be technically inferior. This is due to trace, residual elements of contaminants in the recycled material, or to a fundamental change in the nature of the material as a result of reprocessing. For example, paper fibres are shortened by recycling thus weakening the end product. Recycled plastic, unless taken from a clean, single polymer source, can contain small quantities of unwanted polymers which may affect the performance of the recycled plastic, either in the production of an end product (for example during extrusion) or in the functioning of the end product itself.

While this down-grading of performance is true for some recycled materials it is not true for all. For example the reprocessing of glass and metals produces material which is technically comparable with virgin material. However, before designating recycled material as being technically inferior and therefore second best, we should carefully consider how the reprocessed material is to be used. The question to ask is 'is the material fit for the purpose for which it is intended?'

There are many applications where virgin material actually exceeds the requirements of the product or where minor adjustments to the end product specification would allow recycled material to be used. This applies particularly to products which have low grade uses or for which aesthetics are unimportant. For example, recycled plastic is often unattractively coloured, so any product which is to be buried or hidden, such as pipes or ducting, could be made from recycled plastic such as polyethylene or PVC. This might require the wall thickness of the product to be increased slightly, but for most applications this should not be a problem.

One of the most significant reasons for some recycled materials being cheaper than their virgin alternatives is that the energy required to reprocess the waste material is significantly less than that of converting raw materials into the virgin product. This is true, for example, for glass and for metals. In both cases, the technical comparability of recycled and virgin material and the energy savings associated with recycling have led to these materials achieving the highest levels of recycling, in part by the markets being able to pass on some of the benefit of the energy savings in the payment of relatively high market prices.

Where such energy savings are not available, for example with paper, plastics or textiles recycling, the economic equation can be a very fine balance due to the relatively low value of the recycled material (as in the case of low grade paper) or as a result of the high costs of reprocessing due to technical requirements (as in the case of plastics). In this case, demands from collectors for high prices to be paid by the markets for the recyclable material, can tip this balance so that recycling cannot compete economically with virgin material products.

The barriers to the re-introduction of recycled material into the market place

The biggest single barrier to increasing the use of recycled material is consumer resistance. Whether we are talking about the high-street shopper, commercial buyer or local authority purchasing officer, there is both direct and indirect resistance to the use of recycled materials.

The most obvious example of direct resistance is that pertaining to recycled paper. This exemplifies the two key aspects of such resistance, namely the setting of inappropriate specifications and a lack of understanding. In the case of paper, the inappropriate specification is the belief that exists in this country that all paper should be brilliant white and that any paper which is off-white or coloured is somehow inferior and reflects poorly on the user of such paper.

We should again look at fitness for purpose. While it may be that some organisations believe that high profile documents such as letterheads should be pristine white, that does not mean that internal memos, forms or photocopies also need to be. To quote a Body Shop advertisement 'why aren't all income tax forms, electricity bills, telephone bills, election forms, public notices, newspapers, circular and gas bills printed on recycled paper?'

While the use of recycled paper is increasing, there is still a great deal of resistance based in large part on ignorance. Many users believe recycled paper to be inherently inferior, because the first examples were. They think recycled paper is brown or grey, is absorbent and so cannot be printed on and is generally inferior to the 'real thing'. Nowadays the technology of recycling paper has developed to produce a very wide range of technically competitive, aesthetically pleasing and widely available papers for every purpose. And in most instances recycled paper is not more expensive than virgin. But the misconceptions and prejudices remain and form a significant barrier to the expansion of the markets for recycled material. For many people the word recycled is a synonym for inferior.

As well as direct resistance there is also indirect resistance which causes recycled materials to be unfairly penalised. This is usually as a result of the setting of unnecessarily tight or over-specified standards for material performance, for example, by specifying that fence posts or sign posts must be made of wood, the use of recycled plastic products is precluded, even though such products may in fact be technically superior.

Overcoming resistance

Having identified consumer prejudice as one of the main barriers limiting the growth of the markets for recycled materials, the way to address this barrier is by means of education. Purchasers of all persuasions need to have the relative performance of recycled materials explained and demonstrated to them. We need to explode some of the myths.

Recycled material should be identified as such so that we can all see it in use. For example, the recycled logo on stationery can remind every reader that such paper is available and demonstrates the quality of the product. Plastic and metal containers containing a recycled material content should proclaim the fact, for example carrier bags, bottles or drinks cans. Recycled materials need to be promoted and their quality demonstrated as widely as possible. However, there is a problem that as yet no standard symbols or logos to indicate the recycled or recyclable nature of products have yet been agreed. A proposal for such logos is included in the EU Directive on Packaging and Packaging Waste and are shown in Figures 8.2 and 8.3.

But perhaps the most effective way of overcoming resistance to using recycled materials is to make them cheaper than the virgin equivalent. An analogous situation was that of leaded and unleaded petrol. The environmental arguments in

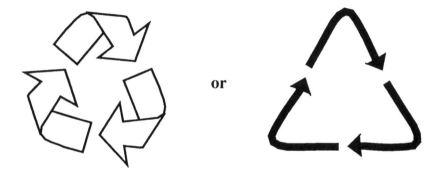

Figure 8.2 Proposed EU logo for recoverable packaging

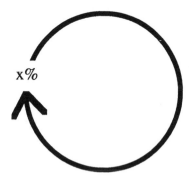

(x% = percentage of recycled material used in the manufacturing of the product)

Figure 8.3 Proposed EU logo for recycled material

favour of using unleaded petrol failed to convince many motorists. It was only the introduction of a price differential in favour of unleaded that made the majority of drivers change so that today, unleaded petrol is the norm. Certainly the situation with petrol was unique in that the government was able to achieve the price differential by a change in duty. Could a similar mechanism be employed using for example, the VAT system, to make products with a recycled material content more competitive? Clearly such a mechanism would potentially be complex and is certainly unlikely in the near future. However, if recyclable materials were to be made available to reprocessors free of charge or at very low prices, and the cost of recycled material thus reduced, such a price differential could be achieved, which brings us back to the central issue of needing to separate markets as reprocessors from the economics of recycling.

Generating consumption

The key to increasing the consumption of products manufactured from recycled materials is therefore to change the purchasing behaviour of all consumers, be they individuals or corporations. Through a process of education and example, consumers can be encouraged to purchase recycled products and more importantly, begin to demand that more products are manufactured either wholly or in part from recycled material. One clear starting point for this process is corporate purchasing, both in the public and the private sector. The purchasing decisions of major corporate bodies have a significant impact on suppliers and the products that they offer. If corporate buyers request or demand an increase in the use of recycled material, it will happen.

Many organisations have started this process by addressing the use of recycled paper, but much more remains to be done. In the UK we consume over 10 million tonnes of paper annually and recycle less than 3.5 million tonnes, with approximately 50 per cent of our paper being imported. By re-assessing the specifications of all paper products, by matching the quality of the product to the purpose for which is required and by setting aside the misconceptions and prejudices regarding recycled paper, a huge increase in the demand for waste paper could be created, leading ultimately to an increase in reprocessing capacity.

The same applies to another significant waste material, plastic. As has already been suggested, there are many applications where recycled plastic could be used, but often, unnecessarily tight product specifications preclude its use. Perhaps there are even opportunities for positive discrimination in favour of recycled material.

Local authorities have a particular role to play in that at present they are leading the development of household waste recycling in the UK. District, borough and county councils are all seeking markets for the recyclable material that they collect. The combined purchasing power of these local authorities is in excess of £4bn per annum. Such purchasing power could be used to great effect. However, if such influence is not used to purchase recycled products, not only is the opportunity lost, but a very clear and negative signal is sent to the markets – 'we want you to take our waste but we are not prepared to buy the end products'. If local authorities are not prepared to buy recycled products, can we expect individuals to?

Local authorities and private sector companies thus have the opportunity to close the recycling loop. An example of this is a scheme operated by Fort Stirling (a paper mill), where local companies collect and supply high grade office waste paper which is reprocessed into tissue products, which the same companies then purchase. Environmental Polymer Products Limited is a major reprocessor of waste plastics but increasingly is requiring local authorities to purchase the company's recycled plastic end-products before they will agree to purchase these authorities' waste plastics for reprocessing.

These are just two examples where the demand for the end-product is being matched to the supply of the waste to be recycled.

There is evidence that corporate purchasers are starting to recognise and to act on this issue. The most high profile evidence was the success of the launch in 1994 by the National Recycling Forum of their 'Buy Recycled Programme', to which an increasing number of organisations are signing up. One of the key objectives of this programme is to publish a comprehensive directory of recycled products which are available so that buyers have a single source of reference when seeking such products.

Conclusion

Markets for recyclable materials can be found today, but it will become increasingly difficult as collected volumes increase. In addition, today's markets do not pay the kind of prices that collectors would like to see. Only if we separate the funding of the collection of recyclable materials from the activity of reprocessing such material, will we see any major expansion in reprocessing capacity in the UK.

If the recyclable materials were to be made available to the markets at little or no cost, capacity would increase dramatically. The potentially stable demand under such circumstances would need to be satisfied by an equally stable supply in terms of volume, quality and frequency of delivering to market. However, such a 'push' approach to the markets is only one half of the solution; the markets also have to be 'pulled' by generating an increased demand for products with a recycled content.

It is therefore the responsibility of all of us, both as individual consumers and as members of purchasing organisations to select, specify and demand that the products we purchase contain whenever possible, materials that have been recycled. It is up to us to close the loop.

CHAPTER NINE

THE COSTS OF RECYCLING

◆

The first bottle bank was introduced over seventeen years ago and ever since, the recycling of household waste has been developing, with the last four to five years having seen a major increase in the level of this activity. It is therefore perhaps a little surprising, given the length of time that recycling has been practised, that one of the most fundamental questions regarding recycling has still not been answered. This is the question: *how much does recycling cost?*

This is not to say that figures for the costs of recycling have not been calculated or published, or to say that the many local authorities who are undertaking recycling collection activities do not know how much they are spending in doing so. Such figures have been prepared in good faith and as accurately as possible, given that much of the data available must often be estimated. The basic problem is, however, that there is no agreed basis for calculating the costs of recycling; there is no standard which defines what costs should be included (and which excluded) or how such costs should be calculated.

The lack of a standard approach has resulted in incomplete or inaccurate cost data being reported, with the risk that this could lead to inappropriate or sub-optimal recycling systems being implemented. All that is really known at present is that recycling costs more than waste disposal: exactly how much more is a matter of debate. A solution to this problem, the proposed Coopers & Lybrand/ERRA costing standard, is presented later in this chapter and the thinking behind it is set out below.

What is the cost of recycling?

Before we can calculate and analyse the costs of recycling, we need to know what costs to include under this heading. For example, the costs of operating a bring collection scheme such as the capital costs of the collection containers and the operating costs of the collection vehicle and crew are clearly all costs of recycling. However, if we consider a kerbside collection scheme which collects both recyclables and refuse, the identification of the costs attributable to recycling and those of refuse collection is less straightforward.

Developing this example further, let the kerbside collection be based on a single, divided wheeled bin and a divided compactor collection vehicle with the division between recyclables and refuse being on the basis of equal volume. The costs of collection attributable to recycling could be calculated on one of two bases:

1) by taking one half of all the collection costs incurred; or
2) by taking only those costs which are incurred, over and above the cost which would have been incurred if there were no recycling.

These two options are illustrated in Figure 9.1

Now, if the kerbside collection had been based on a Blue Box scheme, there would be no problem; the costs of collection for recycling would simply be those of the additional vehicle and crew and of the Blue Box containers, with the costs of the standard refuse collection system remaining unaltered. So with a Blue Box system and as mentioned above with a bring scheme, the costs of collection for recycling are clearly the costs which are incurred, which are additional to those of refuse collection, since in both cases the costs of refuse collection are unchanged. It is both logical and consistent with this approach, that in the case of integrated collection as illustrated in the example above, only the additional costs of collection (the marginal costs) compared to the costs of the standard refuse collection service are attributed to recycling, that is option 2, even though the method of refuse collection may be altered. So in the example illustrated in Figure 9.1, the costs of collection for recycling would be the marginal cost of a divided vehicle compared to a standard vehicle, and the marginal cost of divided wheeled bins compared with standard wheeled bins. There would be no other recycling costs, since for example, the costs of the vehicle crew would be the same as for the standard refuse collection.

A cost of recycling is thus defined as any cost which is incurred which is in addition to the costs which would have been incurred for the standard collection and disposal of household waste. Of course, the introduction of recycling can also lead to reductions in the costs of refuse collection and disposal and this is addressed later in this chapter.

Categories of recycling costs

There are three elements which make up the costs of recycling:

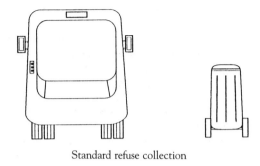

Standard refuse collection

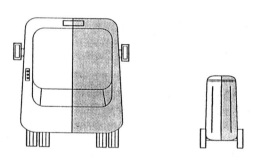

1 Recycling and refuse collection: shared cost

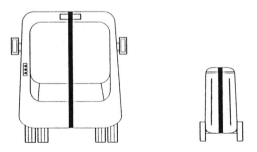

2 Recycling and refuse collection: marginal cost

Figure 9.1 The basis for the cost of recycling

- the cost of collection;
- the cost of processing; and
- the cost of reprocessing.

With regard to the cost of reprocessing collected and sorted material, this cost is essentially reflected in the market price offered by the reprocessing industries. Thus the reprocessing energy savings associated with glass and aluminium recycling are reflected in the relatively high market prices offered for these materials. While there will be some market price distortions, as for example in the case of paper, it is reasonable to take the cost of reprocessing as being addressed within market prices. Any analysis of recycling costs need therefore only consider the costs of collection and processing.

Collection and processing costs are directly linked in an inversely proportional relationship: the greater the degree of separation at source, the greater the cost of collection, but the lower the cost of processing. This relationship is illustrated in Figure 9.2 which shows costs in terms of collection, processing and the combined total, plotted against the degree of separation. Figure 9.2 should be treated as a conceptual rather than a precise representation of the cost relationship. The curves themselves are ill-defined, with data only at the two extremes: a high degree of separation (bring schemes or Blue Box) and for commingled collection (Green Bin). However, the data does confirm that:

1) the costs of collection normally exceed the costs of processing; and
2) there is an optimum degree of separation at source which yields the minimum combined cost of collection and processing.

Experience also confirms the existence of a minimum point on the total cost curve in that, in the Milton Keynes and Adur trials, both of which lie to the left of the graph, are reducing the degree of source separation and thus moving to the right, and experience in Leeds suggests that reintroducing the original divider into the Green Bin to separate paper from the other recyclables, would increase the collection cost but reduce the processing cost, thus moving from the extreme right, further to the left of the graph.

Clearly, in order to plot such a graph and to compare different schemes and methods of collection and processing, a standard method of calculating the costs of recycling is needed.

Units of measurement

One of the basic requirements of any standard is that of agreed units of measurement. Currently there are two units of measurement of recycling costs in common usage:

1) the cost per tonne; and
2) the cost per household.

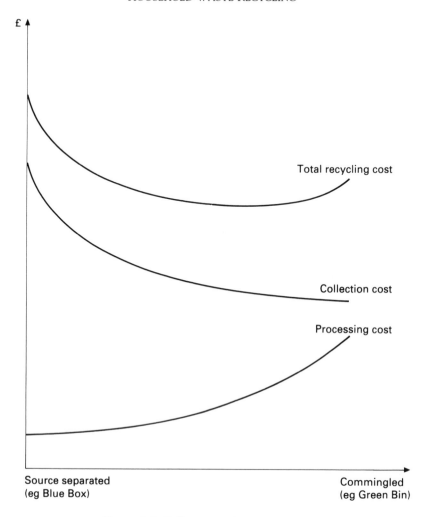

Figure 9.2 Collection and processing costs

Each measure is useful, however a common basis for their calculation is needed. For example, should the cost per tonne be calculated post-collection or post-processing? Equally, should the cost per household be based on participating households only or on all households in a given collection round, regardless of participation?

The following definitions are proposed:

■ *The cost per tonne of recyclable waste* is based on the tonnage of material available for reprocessing following processing.

114

- *The cost per household* is based on the total number of houses in a given collection round, which are participating in the collection of recyclables.

The first definition takes into account not only the quantity but also the quality of the collected material. If collected weight were the basis for measurement, a scheme which had a high degree of collected material rejected during processing would have an artificially low cost per tonne. By using the tonnage of material available after processing this problem does not arise.

The second definition is based on participating households only. If the cost per household were calculated on the basis of all households in a given collection round, irrespective of participation, such a cost figure would only be assessed by reference to the participation rate. For example, let us consider two collection schemes which are identical, apart from one having a lower participation rate, and hence a lower collected tonnage. If the collection cost per household was based on all households in the collection round, the scheme with the lower participation rate would have a higher collection cost per household than the scheme with the higher participation rate, and this figure would change as the participation rate changed. In order to decouple these two factors and to provide a simple basis for comparison between schemes, the cost per household should be based on participating households only.

Using these definitions, the Coopers & Lybrand/ERRA costing standard has been developed and is presented below.

The Coopers & Lybrand/ERRA recycling costing standard

In April 1994 Coopers & Lybrand, in association with ERRA, published a standard approach to calculating the costs of recycling.[40] Such a standard approach is needed, not only to ensure that any particular recycling scheme can be accurately and realistically costed, but in so doing, to allow comparisons between different schemes to be made and alternative approaches to be evaluated.

The development of this standard had three objectives:

1) to determine the true cost of recycling by identifying all of the constituent costs of any recycling scheme and to define a standard reporting structure;
2) to allow consistent and comparable data to be produced on a regular basis (ideally monthly) to provide accurate management information on the performance of a recycling scheme; and
3) to facilitate the comparison of costing data and scheme financial performance between different recycling schemes by calculating and presenting costing data on a consistent basis.

The basis of the standard is the following costing statement.

115

Table 9.1 Total costing statement

Total material sales income		A
Total collection expense	(B)	
Adjustment for collection depreciation	(C_d)	
Less *Total collection costs*		(D)
Total processing expense	(E)	
Adjustment for processing depreciation	(F_d)	
Less *Total processing costs*		(G)
Total recycling cost		(H)

Table 9.2 Calculation of collection costs

		£
Capital expenditure		
Land (premises)		(a)
Land (drop-off sites)		(b)
Buildings		(c)
Collection vehicles		(d)
Collection containers (banks)		(e)
Equipment (collection)		(f)
Equipment (other)		(g)
Promotion (on scheme establishment)		(h)
Total capital expenditure		(C)
Expenses		
Staff costs	– wages and overtime payments	(i)
	– other staff costs	(k)
Transport	– vehicle maintenance and repairs	(l)
	– road tax and insurance	(m)
	– fuel	(n)
	– vehicle hire	(o)
	– other	(p)
Site expenses	– rent and rates	(q)
	– heat, light and power	(r)
	– insurance	(s)
	– maintenance and repair	(t)
Other expenses	– promotional information preparation and distribution	(u)
	– consumables	(v)
	– office supplies and professional services	(w)
	– telephone and postage etc	(x)
	– other	(y)
Total expense		(B)

Collection costs

The collection costs are calculated either for a single collection round or for a scheme as a whole as shown in Table 9.2. The capital costs of collection comprise: the costs of land and buildings (for example for a collection depot) and include any expenditure on land for drop-off sites; the collection vehicles and containers; any other equipment associated with collection; and the promotion costs on the establishment of a new scheme. This last element is included since this is often a significant expenditure item and the benefits of such promotion last beyond the first year of operation. Initial promotional costs are therefore capitalised and depreciated over three years.

The total collection costs (D) are then the sum of the collection expenses (B) and the depreciation on the capital costs of collection (C_d).

Processing costs

The processing costs are calculated on the basis of a discrete processing operation, such as a MRF, irrespective of how many collection rounds feed the processing

Table 9.3 Calculation of processing costs

Capital expenditure		£
Land		(a)
Buildings		(b)
Equipment (processing)		(c)
Equipment (other)		(d)
Total capital expenditure		(F)
Revenue expenses		
Staff costs	– wages and overtime payments	(e)
	– other staff costs	(f)
Site expenses	– rent and rates	(g)
	– heat, light and power	(h)
	– insurance	(i)
	– maintenance and repair	(j)
Process costs	– fuel	(k)
	– consumables	(l)
	– storage	(m)
	– maintenance	(n)
	– waste disposal	(o)
Other expenses	– promotional information preparation and distribution	(p)
	– office supplies and professional services	(q)
	– telephone and postage	(r)
	– other	(s)
Total expense		(E)

operation, as shown in Table 9.3. The capital costs of processing can be significant, in terms of land and buildings and of the equipment involved, particularly if the processing involves a high degree of automation. The capital costs of a typical MRF in the UK are in the range £5–£10m.

The total processing costs (G) are the sum of the depreciated capital cost of processing (F_d) and the associated expenses (E).

The cost of recycling

Having calculated the costs of collection and processing, a cost per tonne needs to be calculated to allow standardised data to be produced. It must be remembered that not all of the material collected will be retained during the processing operation, so that the post-processing tonnage will be less than the collected tonnage. The costs per tonne are calculated as follows:

$$\text{Cost of collection per tonne} = \frac{\text{Total cost of collection (D)}}{\text{Number of tonnes } collected}$$

$$\text{Cost of processing per tonne} = \frac{\text{Total cost of processing (G)}}{\text{Number of tonnes } processed}$$

$$\text{Overall cost per tonne} = \frac{\text{Total cost of collection and total cost of processing (H)}}{\text{Number of tonnes } processed}$$

It should be noted that the combined cost of collection and processed is *not* simply the sum of the cost of collection and the cost of processing. This is illustrated in the following example.

Let the: cost of collection   = £150,000
             cost of processing   = £100,000
             number of tonnes collected = 5000
             processing rate   = 80%

Therefore the: cost of collection

$$= \frac{£150,000}{5000} = £30.00 \text{ per tonne}$$

cost of processing

$$= \frac{£100,000}{5000 \times 0.8} = £25.00 \text{ per tonne}$$

overall recycling cost

$$= \frac{£250,000}{5000 \times 0.8} = £62.50 \text{ per tonne}$$

118

The net cost of recycling

Tables 9.2 and 9.3 and the above discussion of costs per tonne of material report the actual cost of collection and processing. If the collected and processed material is sold for reprocessing and an income received from such sales, when this income is set off against the gross costs of collection and processing, we have the net cost of recycling, since the costs of reprocessing have already been reflected in the price offered for the recyclable material (as discussed above).

Allocation of costs to specific materials

The application of the above method of calculating the costs of recycling is straightforward when applied to a recycling scheme which collects, processes and reprocesses only one material. Examples of such schemes are the collection of glass through glass banks, cans through can banks or some separated organic material through a kerbside scheme. However, when the collection is of commingled materials which have to be separated in a subsequent processing operation, the problem arises of how to allocate the costs of the collection and processing activities to the different materials involved.

The problem is illustrated by the example shown in Table 9.4. Let us take a kerbside scheme which incurs a collection cost of £25 and a processing cost of £40 per tonne of commingled material. We could allocate these total costs on the basis of material volume or by material weight. However, as the table shows, the different bases for cost allocation result in very different costs of recycling per material.

The simple answer to this problem is that there is no single correct basis for the allocation of recycling costs to individual materials in a commingled material scheme. Some methods of allocation are more logical than others, for example, volume is a more appropriate measure for collection, since this is usually the limiting factor, however, in reality whichever unit of measurement is chosen as the basis of allocation, the material being handled must be capable of being measured in this way.

Table 9.4 Allocation of costs by material

	Percentage by volume	Cost allocated by volume (£/tonne)	Percentage by weight	Cost allocated by weight (£/tonne)
Paper	50	32.50	60	39.00
Glass	10	6.50	20	13.00
Aluminium cans	10	6.50	1	0.65
Steel cans	15	9.75	13	8.45
Plastic bottles	15	9.75	6	3.90
TOTAL	100	65.00	100	65.00

Given that there is no single correct basis for allocating costs, what is needed is a universal agreement as to which basis is to be used. This may be difficult to achieve, since different methods of allocation will favour different materials, and the industries associated with each material, notably the packaging industries, will argue for the basis which is most advantageous to their material. For example, allocating costs on the basis of weight rather than volume will reduce the apparent recycling cost per tonne for aluminium cans and plastics, as illustrated in Table 9.4, and vice versa.

This is an area of ongoing research, notably by Coopers & Lybrand, but in the absence of further information and until a common agreement on the basis of cost allocation is reached, a workable proposal based on research conducted in the USA[41] is to allocate costs as follows:

- direct allocation of a cost if only one material is involved, for example labour or equipment which is handling only one material;
- pro-rata allocation on the basis of material weight for equipment used for mixed materials, such as conveyors and for sorting staff;
- allocation by time usage for resources which are used for more than one seg-regated material, for example if a baler is used 50 per cent of the time for baling plastics and 50 per cent for metals; and
- allocation on the basis of material volume for items such as building storage space.

Avoided collection and disposal savings

As was mentioned earlier in this chapter, the introduction of recycling can result in decreases in the costs of refuse collection and will result in decreases in the costs of waste disposal. For example, the introduction of intensive bring collection schemes or of a Blue Box kerbside collection scheme could reduce the amount of the remaining refuse to be collected so much that the weekly collection of refuse could be reduced to a fortnightly collection, with an obvious reduction in refuse collection costs. This poses the question as to whether such a saving, the so-called avoided collection saving, should be attributed to recycling or to refuse collection. The same question arises when savings arise as a result of avoiding disposal as a result of recycling.

This concept of avoided collection and disposal savings is one which is often misunderstood. The argument for avoided collection and disposal savings being attributed to recycling is based on the fact that if no other method of waste management is used, waste will always have to be collected and disposed of. Waste disposal is thus the base method of waste treatment and the costs of refuse collection and disposal are the base costs which will be incurred. If a system of recycling is introduced which reduces this base cost in terms of collection and/or disposal, then it is argued that this saving should be credited to the new recycling system. However, what must be clearly understood is that this approach simply identifies the relative costs of the two methods of waste management.

This is best explained by way of example. Taking the case of collection first, let us assume the following:

1) a weekly cost of £500 for the collection of 10 tonnes of refuse;
2) a weekly cost of £200 for the kerbside collection of 2.5 tonnes of recycling material; and
3) a cost of £750 if 15 tonnes of refuse were collected once per fortnight.

In the situation where there is no recycling, the refuse collection cost for a two week period would be £1000. If kerbside recycling were introduced, the collection cost for the same period would be £750 for refuse collection and £400 for recyclables collection – a total of £1150.

The earlier definition of a cost of recycling is any cost which is incurred which is in addition to the costs which would have been incurred for the standard collection of household refuse. In this example therefore, the collection cost for recycling is £1150 minus £1000 or £150. If we now consider the concept of a collection saving, we can see from this example that the cost of refuse collection will be reduced from £1000 to £750, a saving of £250. This saving arises as a direct result of the introduction of recycling, so it would seem reasonable to credit this saving against the cost of recycling collection of £400, giving the same cost of recycling of £150.

Let us now examine an example relating to recycling and disposal. Let us assume the following:

1) 10 tonnes of waste to be treated;
2) a disposal cost of £20 per tonne;
3) a recycling processing cost of £45 per tonne; and
4) 2 tonnes of the 10 tonnes of waste is recyclable.

In the situation where there is no recycling, the cost of disposal would be £200. With recycling, the cost of disposal would be £160 and of processing £90, a total of £250. Again using the above definition of a cost of recycling, the processing cost of recycling would be £250 minus £200 or £50. Equally, the saving is disposal costs would be £40, which when credited against the £90 cost of processing, gives a cost of processing of £50.

Both of these examples show that the definition of a cost of recycling being any cost which is incurred, which is in addition to the costs which would have been incurred for the standard collection and disposal of household refuse, automatically takes into account any collection and disposal savings which arise as a result of recycling.

What these two examples also clearly demonstrate is that this definition and the concept of collection and disposal savings, report the cost of recycling *relative* to those of the basic refuse collection and disposal service. This is not the same as the absolute cost of recycling. In the two examples above, the absolute cost of collection for recycling is £400 for two weeks and the relative cost £150, and the absolute cost of processing is £45 per tonne, compared with the relative cost of £25 per tonne.

If we are considering the absolute cost of recycling, therefore, any collection or disposal savings are ignored. If, however, we are interested in the cost of recycling relative to that of disposal, then collection and disposal savings are credited against the absolute cost of recycling. In general, when people talk about the cost of recycling, it is the latter to which they are referring and it is the latter which has been defined as the cost of recycling in this chapter. The only time that the absolute costs of recycling are important is when for example a number of recycling schemes are being compared and differences between the schemes in terms of the base costs of refuse collection or disposal could distort the comparison of recycling costs.

The cost of recycling is one measure of the performance of a recycling scheme. While it is very important, it is not the only measure of performance. In the next chapter we examine other measures, and identify ways in which the cost of recycling and these other performance measures can be combined.

CHAPTER TEN

MEASURING RECYCLING PERFORMANCE

◆

Diversion rate

The key measure of success of any recycling scheme is the amount of material which is diverted from the normal disposal route. This is usually expressed as a percentage. For example, the government's target is to divert 25 per cent of all household waste from disposal routes by recycling the waste instead of burying or burning it, and this target is to be achieved by the year 2000.

The term 'recycling rate' is now in common usage to express this measure of performance, so that the government's target is often described as achieving a 25 per cent recycling rate by the year 2000. However, the way that the performance of recycling is currently measured means that this term is incorrect. It is relatively easy to weigh the materials *collected* for recycling and it is relatively easy to weigh the materials that have been *processed* prior to reprocessing. Such measurements are also taken sufficiently close to the point of arising, for the total weight of the associated waste steam to be known. The percentage of the waste stream collected for recycling can thus be calculated, as can the percentage of material processed for recycling. However, it is not normally possible to measure the weight of material actually recycled, that is, collected, processed and *reprocessed*, in relation to the weight of the original waste stream. The term recycling rate is thus a misnomer, particularly since it is usually measured after collection only. Anyone who currently reports their recycling rate is actually reporting the percentage of the waste stream collected for the purposes of recycling.

For example, the DoE has defined the local authority recycling rate[42] as:

$$\text{Local authority recycling rate} = \frac{\text{total weight of designated recyclables collected and available for recycling}}{\text{total weight of designated recyclables available for recycling}}$$

The government's target for this ratio is 50 per cent and if the denominator is replaced by the total weight of household waste, the target becomes 25 per cent.

We therefore need to define a term which accurately describes what is being measured. If the measurement is taken after collection, an accurate description would be the 'collection rate for recycling'. If the measurement is made after collection and processing, this can be described as the 'diversion rate for recycling', that is, the percentage of the waste stream diverted from disposal for the purposes of recycling. We could equally define the 'diversion rate for recovery'.

While the collection rate is easy to measure and is of some interest, it is the diversion rate which is of greater importance. This is because it is a measure, not only of the quantity of material collected for recycling, but also of the quality of that material. The processing stage of the recycling process selects only those materials suitable for reprocessing. A recycling scheme which collects a large percentage of the waste stream for recycling, but which collects a large proportion of unsuitable or contaminated materials, will have a high collection rate, but a much lower diversion rate, reflecting the poor quality of the collected materials. Since we cannot accurately measure the recycling rate, we should measure and report the diversion rate as the most accurate indicator of a recycling scheme's performance.

In order to define this and other performance measures, we need to define the size of the waste stream with which a given recycling scheme is associated. We all generate waste and it is collected from us on the basis of individual households. The waste stream can therefore be defined as the total amount of waste generated by a given number of households. The size of the waste stream associated with a particular recycling scheme, is, then, the total amount of waste generated by the households served by that recycling scheme.

We can thus define the diversion rate for the households served by a recycling scheme as the:

$$\text{diversion rate (for recycling)} = \frac{\text{weight of material collected and processed}}{\text{total weight of waste generated}}$$

Any recycling scheme is designed to collect only certain materials. For example a bring scheme may be set up to collect glass, newspapers and magazines and metal cans. Equally, a kerbside scheme might be established to collect paper and board, rigid and film plastics, metal cans and textiles. The materials to be collected by a given scheme are specific to that scheme and are referred to as 'targeted' materials.

If we know the quantity of targeted materials in the waste steam, we can also define the potential diversion rate as the:

$$\text{potential diversion rate (for recycling)} = \frac{\text{weight of targeted material generated}}{\text{total weight of waste generated}}$$

The effectiveness of the diversion can then be expressed as the:

$$\text{diversion effectiveness} = \frac{\text{diversion rate}}{\text{potential diversion rate}}$$

For example, let us consider a kerbside scheme which has been designed to target all paper and board, steel cans, aluminium cans and foil and rigid plastics, but not plastic film. Table 10.1 reproduces average data for these arisings from Waste Management Paper 28.[43] This shows both the gross arisings and estimates of how much of this material is suitable for recycling.

Table 10.1 Average material arisings (per household per annum)

Material	Gross arisings (kg)	Recyclable arisings (kg)
Paper and board	200	120
Steel cans	42	34
Aluminium cans and foil	4	3
Rigid plastics	18	13
TOTAL	264	170

Taking the weight of all waste as 600kg per household per annum, this would give a potential diversion rate based on the gross arisings of 44 per cent. If all of the estimated recyclable material was collected and processed, the actual diversion rate would be 28 per cent, giving a diversion effectiveness of 64 per cent.

The above definition of the diversion rate allows us to measure the performance not only of recycling schemes, but also of recovery schemes. To recall the definition of recovery in Chapter 1:

Recovery means to recycle, compost, regenerate or to extract the energy to be used as an energy source

We can therefore also define a measure of the performance of a recovery scheme as the:

$$\text{diversion rate (for recovery)} = \frac{\text{amount of material diverted}}{\text{total amount of waste generated}}$$

If such a scheme were based wholly on energy recovery through incineration, the potential diversion rate would be 100 per cent, but the actual diversion rate would be lower, reflecting the fact that not all of the waste sent for incineration would be combustible, resulting in a residue requiring disposal. As we saw in Chapter 4, recycling can be successfully used to divert such materials prior to incineration, and the more this were achieved, the closer the diversion effectiveness (for recovery) would be to 100 per cent.

When defining performance ratios we need to be careful in the use of the terms which are used to describe these ratios. For example, the ERRA definition of the diversion rate refers to recovery as.[44]

$$\text{diversion rate (household waste)} = \frac{\text{amount of material recovered from generators served}}{\text{total amount of available waste from generators served}}$$

and is applied at the end of the final process, prior to sale to the end market, for example at the output from a MRF. In this instance recovery is used to mean collection and processing, rather than in the sense of the above definition of recovery. To avoid confusion the use of the term 'recovery' should be limited to the above definition, and by using the more specific description of 'collection and processing', the need to define the point of application of the ratio becomes unnecessary as this is self-evident.

Householder participation

In the UK, recycling schemes are voluntary: only those householders who wish to, actually take part. A secondary measure of the success of a scheme is therefore the percentage of participation of the householders who are served by the scheme. The measure of how many householders put out their recyclables container for collection on any given collection day is defined as the:

$$\text{set-out rate} = \frac{\text{number of households putting out the container on a given collection day}}{\text{number of households served by the scheme on that collection day}}$$

With some schemes, such as Blue Box kerbside, householders may participate, but not every week. In order to ensure that we measure all householders who take part in the scheme on a reasonably frequent basis, the following measure has been defined:

$$\text{Participation rate} = \frac{\text{number of households participating at least once in a four-week period}}{\text{total number of households served by the scheme}}$$

Clearly it is the objective of any recycling scheme to maximise both the set-out rate and the participation rate. In other words, not only do we want as many householders as possible to participate at least once every four weeks, but we want as many as possible to set out their container for collection *every* week. In theory, it is possible to have a 100 per cent participation rate with only a 25 per cent set-out rate.

The set-out rate is clearly more easily measured than the participation rate, since the number of containers set out for collection on any given day is simply counted as the containers are emptied by the collection vehicle. Research in the USA has suggested that there is a relationship between the participation rate and the set-out rate, which can be used to estimate the participation rate, if only the set-out rate is known. This research indicates that the participation rate is 2 or 2.5 times the set-out rate for weekly programmes, 1.5 for fortnightly programmes and, not surprisingly, 1 for monthly programmes. Data from a scheme in Sheffield and a scheme in Devon supports these figures.[45]

The monitoring of the set-out rate and participation rate over time is important in order to identify any changes in householder behaviour. The most common occurrence is for one or both rates to decline as householders' enthusiasm for source separation is reduced. By measuring, in particular the participation rate (either directly or calculated from the set-out rate), any decline can be highlighted, and measures such as educational or promotional activities initiated, in order to increase the level of support for the scheme.

As well as measuring householder participation levels, it is also important to measure the quality of that participation. To do this we need to measure the amount of targeted material being collected, which is defined as the:

$$\text{collection effectiveness} \ = \ \frac{\begin{array}{c}\text{amount of targeted material collected from} \\ \text{all households served}\end{array}}{\begin{array}{c}\text{total amount of targeted material generated} \\ \text{by the households served}\end{array}}$$

This should not be confused with the collection rate which was discussed earlier and which measures the percentage of the total waste stream collected for recycling. The collection effectiveness is rather a measure of how much of the targeted material is actually being collected. In order to relate this to the level of householder participation, a measure of the quality of participating householders has been defined as the:

$$\text{capture rate} \ = \ \frac{\begin{array}{c}\text{amount of targeted material collected per} \\ \text{participating household}\end{array}}{\begin{array}{c}\text{total amount of targeted material generated} \\ \text{by each household served}\end{array}}$$

Alternatively, this is expressed as the:

$$\frac{\dfrac{\begin{array}{c}\text{amount of targeted material collected from} \\ \text{all households served}\end{array}}{\begin{array}{c}\text{number of households participating at} \\ \text{least once in a four week period}\end{array}}}{\dfrac{\begin{array}{c}\text{total amount of targeted material generated} \\ \text{by all households served}\end{array}}{\begin{array}{c}\text{total number of households served by the} \\ \text{scheme}\end{array}}}$$

127

which is the same as the:

$$\frac{\dfrac{\text{amount of targeted material collected from}}{\text{all households served}}}{\dfrac{\text{total amount of targeted material generated}}{\text{by all households served}}}$$

$$\frac{\dfrac{\text{number of households participating at}}{\text{least once in a four week period}}}{\dfrac{\text{total number of households served by the}}{\text{scheme}}}$$

Thus, the:

$$\text{capture rate} = \frac{\text{collection effectiveness}}{\text{participation rate}}$$

A worked example

Let us examine a kerbside scheme which is used to collect paper and board, rigid plastics and steel and aluminium cans on a weekly basis.

The following data is available:

- Number of households served : 20,000 households
- Total waste arisings : 230 tonnes per week
- Weight of targeted materials in : 5.5 kg per household per week
  waste stream
- Weight of recyclables collected : 50 tonnes per week
- Measured set-out rate : 28 per cent of households
- Processing effectiveness : 90 per cent of collected material

From this data, the performance of the scheme can be analysed as follows:

$$\text{Diversion rate} = \frac{50 \times 0.9}{230} = 20 \text{ per cent}$$

$$\text{Potential diversion rate} = \frac{0.0055 \times 20,000}{230} = 48 \text{ per cent}$$

This performance can be compared with the government's recycling target. This target is based on 50 per cent of household waste being recyclable (compared with the above potential diversion rate of 48 per cent) and 50 per cent of this fraction actually being recycled (compared with the above diversion effectiveness of 41 per cent).

This can be further analysed by examining the performance of the households, as follows:

Participation rate	$= 2.5 \times 28$		$= 70$ per cent
Collection effectiveness	$= \dfrac{50}{0.0055 \times 20,000}$		$= 45$ per cent
Capture rate	$= \dfrac{45}{70}$		$= 64$ per cent

Bring schemes

All of the preceding performance indicators apply equally to kerbside and to bring collection schemes, however there are problems with measuring some of these ratios for bring schemes.

The key problem is defining the catchment area of a drop-off site. The DoE[46] have defined the density of drop-off sites as:

$$\text{Drop-off site density} = \frac{\text{number of households in the catchment area}}{\text{number of drop-off sites for each designated recyclable}}$$

The Civic Amenity Waste Disposal Project (CAWDP) has proposed that a drop-off site be defined as any site containing any number of banks, within a 50m radius,[47] and suggests that the catchment area should be defined in terms of the number of households or population within a given local authority. This is a workable basis for estimating the population served by such schemes, but it must be recognised that this is only an estimation, since the actual usage of such drop-off facilities will not be limited to those people living within the particular local authority. In addition, such an approach does not allow the performance of individual drop-off sites to be measured, which in terms of the selection of site location and day-to-day management, is of at least equal importance.

The DoE has also defined a drop-off site participation rate and a drop-off site yield[46] as follows:

$$\begin{array}{l}\text{Drop-off site} \\ \text{participation rate}\end{array} = \frac{\begin{array}{c}\text{number of households using a drop-off site} \\ \text{at least once in a four week period}\end{array}}{\begin{array}{c}\text{number of households in the drop-off site} \\ \text{catchment area}\end{array}}$$

$$\begin{array}{l}\text{Drop-off site yield of} \\ \text{designated recyclables}\end{array} = \frac{\begin{array}{c}\text{total weight of each designated recyclable for} \\ \text{all drop-off sites in a programme}\end{array}}{\begin{array}{c}\text{number of households offered the drop-off} \\ \text{site programme}\end{array}}$$

It is acknowledged within the definition that participation will be difficult to measure (the only method would be by periodic surveys of site users) and that the denominator of the yield is difficult to monitor.

The need for waste analysis

In order to measure the performance of a recycling scheme we have to take certain measurements, some of which are easier to obtain than others. Table 10.2 summarises the key performance ratios and it is clear that these measurements fall into two categories:

1) Factors which need to be measured on a day-to-day basis, such as the weight of recyclables collected and processed or the number of households setting-out or participating; and
2) Factors which only need to be measured periodically, such as the number of households served by the scheme or the amount of targeted material generated by the households served.

Table 10.2 Summary of recycling performance indicators

Performance indicator	Definition
Collection rate	$\dfrac{\text{weight of material collected for recycling}}{\text{total weight of waste generated}}$
Diversion rate	$\dfrac{\text{weight of material collected and processed}}{\text{total weight of waste generated}}$
Potential diversion rate	$\dfrac{\text{weight of targeted material generated}}{\text{total weight of waste generated}}$
Diversion effectiveness	$\dfrac{\text{diversion rate}}{\text{potential diversion rate}}$
Set-out rate	$\dfrac{\text{number of households putting out the container on a given collection day}}{\text{number of households served by the scheme on that collection day}}$
Participation rate	$\dfrac{\text{number of households participating at least once in a four week period}}{\text{total number of households served by the scheme}}$
Collection effectiveness	$\dfrac{\text{amount of targeted material collected from all households served}}{\text{total amount of targeted material generated by the households served}}$
Capture rate	$\dfrac{\text{amount of targeted material collected per participating household}}{\text{total amount of targeted material generated by each household}}$

In order to calculate the ratios listed in Table 10.2, we need to take the following measurements:

1) the weight of material collected (and processed);
2) the total weight of waste generated;
3) the weight of targeted material generated (for all households served and for each participating household);
4) the number of households setting out or participating;
5) the number of households served (on a given collection day and by the scheme in total);
6) the amount of target material collected (from all households and from all participating households).

Items 1) and 2) are readily obtained from collection vehicle weighbridge records (while not all refuse collection is currently weighed, this is increasingly the case and is certainly the case for recyclables collection). Item 4) needs to be periodically measured and item 5) is essentially fixed. This leaves item 3), the weight of targeted materials generated and item 6), the amount of targeted material collected.

The required information on targeted materials can only be obtained by the use of wastestream analyses, which establish the amount and composition of samples of the waste arisings. A number of analysis techniques are available, two of which are used in the National Household Waste Analysis Project[48] and that advocated by ERRA.[49]

An annual (or more frequent) wastestream analysis which identifies the typical composition of the waste arisings can form the basis of calculating item 3), once the total amount of waste generated is known. Indeed, the work of the National Household Waste Analysis Project may itself provide this composition data. However, item 6), the amount of targeted material collected, can only be measured by analysing samples of collected material, which is clearly a costly and time-consuming process.

When designing a recycling scheme, it is vital that such a wastestream analysis is undertaken in order to identify what is the wastestream, in terms of both the composition and the arisings of potentially recyclable materials. Only when this information is known can the most appropriate collection and processing methods be designed and the performance targets for the scheme be set.

Establishing recycling scheme targets

The process of establishing the performance targets for a recycling scheme is relatively simple, as is the subsequent monitoring of performance that should be undertaken.

The starting point is to decide the number of households to be served by the scheme and the materials which are to be collected (the targeted materials). The *potential diversion rate* can then be assessed, which will require a wastestream analysis to be carried out to establish the weight of targeted material generated, compared with the total weight of waste generated. Once the potential diversion rate has been calculated, the range of targeted materials can be reviewed and increased or decreased, to ensure that the scheme will have a potential diversion rate which is acceptable.

An assessment should then be made of the likely *participation rate*, based on the proposed methods of collection and any existing data on past or current levels of householder participation in recycling schemes. For example, in an area where there has been a history of recycling, participation could be expected to be higher than one where recycling is completely new. Evidence of participation rates from similar schemes elsewhere should also be taken into account.

The likely participation rate, together with the weight of targeted material generated by each household served (from the wastestream analysis) will allow a target *collection rate* to be set, and with an estimate of the processing efficiency, for a target *diversion rate* to be set. Targets for both the *collection and diversion effectiveness* will then follow.

Once the scheme is established, the collection rate and diversion rate should be regularly monitored and compared with the targets set. If performance is below these targets, the reasons for the under-performance can be established by reviewing the actual *participation rate*, to see if the problem is one of not enough households taking part in the scheme, and the *capture rate* to establish whether the problem is one of having a sufficient number of households participating, but each household not separating a sufficient quantity of the targeted materials. Once the cause of the problem is known, appropriate action can be taken.

Performance measurement

It is vital that we are able to measure the performance of any recycling scheme, both in order to design appropriate schemes, and to ensure that they perform to the targets set. The performance measures defined above allow this information to be generated using measurements, which apart from the need for waste stream analyses, are relatively straightforward to obtain. However, the need for periodic wastestream analysis should not be underestimated, and the cost of this work should be included within the budget of any recycling scheme.

As part of the design of a recycling scheme, appropriate and sufficiently wide-spread wastestream analyses should be undertaken and targets set for all of the above performance measures, to ensure that the design of the scheme is capable of delivering the diversion rate required. Once established, it is vital that performance is regularly monitored and if the high level measures indicate that a problem is developing, then more specific measures can then be used to highlight the problem, to allow appropriate action to be taken.

Experience has shown that any recycling scheme needs some degree of ongoing support to ensure its continued performance. Careful initial design and regular monitoring will allow such support to be targeted and hence effective, thus maximising the chances of success.

The cost of recycling and other performance measures

In this chapter we have examined measures which report various technical aspects of a recycling scheme's performance. In the previous chapter we analysed the cost of recycling and showed how this can be reported on the basis of a cost per tonne of material handled.

In order to fully understand and analyse any given recycling scheme, these two sets of measures need to be brought together. For example let us take the two schemes summarised in Table 10.3.

Scheme A clearly has the higher diversion rate, but Scheme B incurs the lower cost. So which scheme has the superior performance? This is only revealed when we examine the composite measure of the cost per tonne per percentage point of diversion as follows:

$$\text{Cost per tonne per percentage point of diversion} = \frac{\text{Cost per tonne}}{\text{recycling diversion rate}}$$

Applying this measure to the examples in Table 10.3 shows that Scheme A has the more cost effective performance (£2.17 per tonne per percentage point of diversion) compared with £2.37 per tonne per percentage point of diversion for Scheme B.

By combining the two key measures of performance of cost and diversion rate in this way, we can report a composite measure which reflects the cost effectiveness of any recycling Scheme, with such effectiveness being measured in terms of the amount of waste diverted from disposal, which as stated at the start of this chapter, is the key measure of technical performance of any recycling scheme.

Table 10.3 Recycling scheme performance examples

Scheme	Net cost (£/tonne)	Recycling Diversion Rate (%)
A	50	23
B	45	19

CHAPTER ELEVEN

PACKAGING AND PACKAGING WASTE

———————◆———————

Of all the materials contained in household waste, discarded packaging is seen by many people as representing both the worst aspects of our consumption and disposal culture and the greatest opportunity for recycling. Waste packaging accounts for approximately 30 per cent by weight and by volume of all household waste, as may be seen from Table 11.1.[50] Indeed, packaging accounts for the majority of the dry recyclable elements of household waste in terms of cardboard, glass, plastics and metals, the other major non-packaging element being newspapers and magazines. Packaging is thus a significant element of household waste, but has received a level of criticism which is perhaps disproportionate to the amount of packaging which is actually discarded.

This focus on packaging as a target for waste minimisation and recycling is in part due to its voluminous nature and thus high visibility (this being particularly true of plastics) and partly due to the widely held public perception that many goods are over-packaged. We will therefore begin our study of this subject by examining the nature and the role of packaging today.

Why we need packaging

Virtually every product that we purchase today is packaged. The design of the packaging and the material used will vary greatly from product to product,

Table 11.1 Packaging in household waste

Material	Packaging type	Percentage of total waste by weight	by volume[4]
Paper and board	Liquid containers	0.6	
	Board packaging	3.8	9.1
	Other board[1]	3.1	
Plastics	Film[2]	4.1	10.3
	Beverage bottles	0.7	
	Other bottles	1.1	8.0
	Food packaging	1.9	
Glass	Clear	5.4	
	Green	2.4	2.0
	Brown	1.3	
Ferrous metal	Beverage cans	0.5	
	Food cans	3.7	1.5
	Other cans	0.4	
Non-ferrous metal[3]	Beverage cans	0.4	
	Foil[2]	0.5	0.9
TOTAL		29.9	31.8

1 Includes an estimated small percentage of non-packaging board; 2 These categories will include a proportion of non-packaging film and foil such as material used in domestic cooking; 3 Miscellaneous non-ferrous metals represent an additional 0.7% of the waste stream and include some packaging items such as milk bottle tops; 4 Based on estimates of bulk density

reflecting the role which the packaging has been designed to perform. Packaging is required to fulfil the following functions:

- to provide protection from physical damage, contamination and deterioration;
- to provide sales appeal, identify the brand and promote the product;
- to give information on the product content, composition and use;
- to optimise distribution and storage costs;
- to provide consumer convenience, for example the provision of individual food portions; and
- to fulfil a safety function in preventing product tampering or inappropriate use, for example child-proof tops on medicine bottles.

There are three levels of packaging:

1) **Sales or primary packaging** is the packaging associated with a product at the point of sale to the consumer; it is what we take with us when we leave a shop.
2) **Grouping or secondary packaging** is that used to combine primary sales units into a larger pack, either for sale to the consumer or to assist in store shelf replenishment.

3) **Transport or tertiary packaging** is the packaging used to pack goods in bulk for transportation and to protect such goods in transit.

In order to meet the many and sometimes conflicting requirements placed on packaging, as outlined above, packaging designers have produced increasingly sophisticated packaging techniques which have sought to maximise the function and the appeal of the packaging, while minimising cost. Until relatively recently, little consideration has been given either to the environmental impact of the packaging or its ultimate disposal. The drive to minimise cost has, however, led indirectly to improvements in the environmental performance of packaging. For example, one of the prime functions of packaging is to protect goods in transit. Packaged goods are transported considerable distances and much effort has been expended on minimising the costs of such transport. When transporting goods there is a clear financial incentive to maximise the amount of product being transported and to minimise the amount of packaging. This has been the impetus behind a continued process of packaging lightweighting which has resulted in the amount of packaging per unit product being reduced in recent years: clearly an example of waste minimisation in practice, albeit unintentionally.

The EU Directive on Packaging and Packaging Waste

One example of the focus of attention on packaging as a target for recycling is the recently adopted EC Directive on Packaging and Packaging Waste. This directive will replace earlier Commission attempts to legislate on the recovery of packaging, notably the 1985 directive on Containers for Liquids for Human Consumption (85/339/EEC).

This directive covers a wide range of issues such as the setting of targets, the marking of packaging to indicate whether it is made from recycled and/or recyclable material, waste packaging return and management systems and the establishment of a European packaging database. The key feature of the directive is the targets that it sets for packaging recycling and recovery. Originally, within ten years of the directive being implemented by member states, 90 per cent of packaging waste was to be recovered (with 60 per cent being recycled as material) and only 10 per cent being allowed to go to landfill, and then only after this material had been through either a recycling or recovery process. The directive was not prescriptive as to how such targets are to be achieved. The targets were clearly very high and did not differentiate between different packaging materials. Thus, for glass and metals (for which energy recovery is not an option) the target was effectively 90 per cent material recycling. Even though energy recovery is an option for paper, board and plastics, the 60 per cent material recycling target for these materials was considered by many people to be excessive.

The final form of the directive however contains a revised set of targets, as follows:

■ an overall recovery rate of 60 per cent;

- a recycling rate of between 25 per cent and 45 per cent; and
- a minimum recycling rate for each material of 15 per cent.

These targets are to be achieved within five years. Clearly there are a number of significant changes. First, the overall level of recovery has been significantly reduced as has the minimum level of recycling (from 60 per cent to 25 per cent). Secondly, a maximum level of recycling has been specified, which may only be exceeded if the member state concerned has sufficient recycling capacity to reprocess the material. Thirdly, a minimum recycling rate has been set for each material. The directive takes no account of, and does not give any credit for, waste minimisation. The fact that there is no incentive for packaging manufacturers to reduce the amount of packaging used and discarded is a major criticism of the directive.

One of the justifications for the directive put forward by the European Commission is the need to harmonise the actions being taken on packaging by individual member states and in particular, to avoid distortions to the single market. Of the twelve member states, three (Germany, France and the Netherlands) have already taken significant action on packaging. Italy has introduced limited actions and Belgium is in the process of implementing packaging legislation. So far the remaining seven countries (including Britain) have taken little or no action.

The actions taken by the four leading member states are summarised below.

Germany

The Packaging Ordinance of 12 June 1991 is the most prescriptive and demanding piece of legislation passed by any European government with regard to packaging waste. The key element of the ordinance is the obligation imposed on manufacturers and distributors to take back waste packaging for reuse or recycling *independently* of the public waste management system.

A series of key dates was set out in the ordinance:

- from 1 December 1991 industry was to take back and reuse or recycle all transport packaging;
- from 1 April 1992 consumers would have the right to leave all sales packaging with the retailer at the time of purchase; and
- from 1 January 1993 retailers would be obliged to take back for the purpose of reuse or recycling, used primary packaging, either in their shop or at a collection point in close proximity.

A DM0.50 obligatory deposit on single-trip beverage, washing product and paint containers was also introduced from 1 January 1993.

A counter-proposal from industry lead to the creation of the now famous Duales System Deutschland (DSD). This is a non-profit making national organisation set up to organise and fund the collection, processing and reprocessing of waste packaging. DSD lets contracts for the collection and processing of used

Table 11.2 DSD packaging levy rates

Material	Levy (Pfennigs per kilogramme)
Glass	16
Paper and board	33
Steel cans	56
Aluminium cans	100
Plastic	300
Composites[1]	166

1 For example drinks cartons

packaging and makes the sorted materials available to the reprocessing industries free of charge.

DSD is funded by licensing the use of 'der Grüne Punkt', the 'Green Dot' logo. Licensed companies are entitled to use the Green Dot on their packaging in return for the payment of a licence fee based initially on the rates shown in Table 11.2.

An additional fee of 0.5 Pfennig is charged for plastic packaging. It was the intention that retailers would only stock products carrying the Green Dot and that consumers would purchase such products in preference to others, having been convinced that such packaging was more environmentally acceptable.

The costs of DSD were originally calculated to be DM2000m per annum or an average of 2 Pfennig per package for 100 billion packages. The German government agreed to the creation of DSD, but required the quotas set out in Table 11.3 to be achieved.

DSD commenced operations on 1 July 1991 with plans to bring five million inhabitants into the scheme every three months.

The waste packaging collection is by a combination of bring and kerbside schemes as illustrated in Figure 11.1. Glass is collected using glass banks and is colour separated at source; cardboard and packaging papers are also collected at drop-off sites. Metal cans, aluminium foil, drinks cartons, plastics and composite

Table 11.3 DSD recycling quotas

Material	By 01/01/93 (%)			By 01/07/95 (%)		
	Collection[1]	Sorting	Recycling	Collection	Sorting	Recycling
Glass	60	70	42	80	90	72
Tinplate steel	40	65	26	80	90	72
Aluminium	30	60	18	80	90	72
Cardboard	30	60	18	80	80	64
Paper	30	60	18	80	80	64
Plastic	30	30	9	80	80	64
Composites	20	30	6	80	80	64

1 The quotas specified for each individual packaging material shall be deemed to have been met if at least 50 per cent of the total packaging material accumulated has been collected for recycling

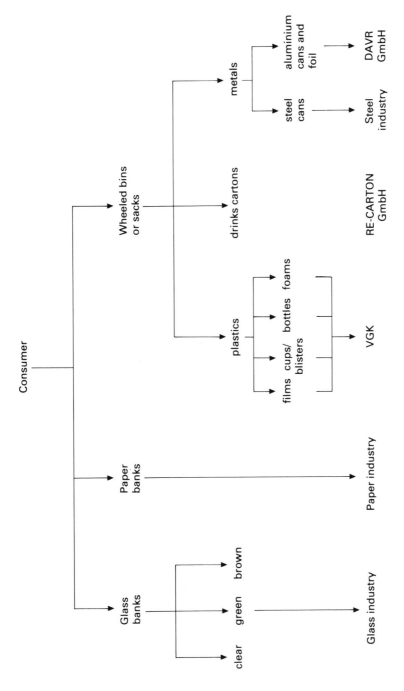

Figure 11.1 Duales System Deutschland (DSD)

materials such as blister packs are collected using kerbside schemes, based on yellow wheeled bins or sacks. The commingled materials are taken to sorting plants for separation.

There has been much criticism of the operation of DSD, primarily because the very large quantities of packaging materials collected could not be processed by the German reprocessing industries. In order to meet the very tough collection quotas, DSD had to collect material whether or not there was a market for it. As a consequence, post-consumer packaging materials were 'dumped' by DSD in neighbouring European countries. Sorted packaging waste was supplied either free of charge or in the case of plastics, the reprocessors were paid to accept DSD derived material. This flooding of the European reprocessing markets with free or subsidised material dealt a major blow to the existing reprocessing infrastructures in a number of European countries, including Britain.

In addition to such criticism, DSD has faced increasing financial difficulties. The original annual budget estimate of DM2 billion was soon shown to be inaccurate; the budget for 1994 was DM4.2 billion and rising. This was partly due to the collection quotas which were set. In order to meet these quotas, DSD had to accept almost any contract which they were offered, since they were not in a strong position to negotiate keen contract prices.

In September 1993, DSD faced a crisis. The company owed its collection and sorting contractors between DM600–800 million. The contractors threatened to cease collection unless paid. At a last minute meeting with the Environment Minister Dr Töpfer, the debt was converted to a long-term credit from the collection contractors, who became members of DSD itself. While this resolved the situation, it also focused attention on the primary problem that DSD was facing and which was a fundamental weakness of the whole design of the scheme. The packaging companies were suspected of deliberately understating the number of packages that they sold in order to avoid paying the Green Dot licence fee, hence starving DSD of funds.

The weakness which this highlighted was that the ultimate threat of the Packaging Ordinance, the 'take-back obligation' was aimed at the retailers, who understandably wanted the scheme to succeed. The Green Dot licence fee, however, was paid by the packaging producers, who were not subject to the same threat and who, it would appear, were less committed to the success of DSD.

As a result of the criticism that DSD and the Packaging Ordinance has faced, the German government is proposing to amend the original legislation. The original quotas shown in Table 11.3 are to be slightly reduced and an additional three years will be given for their achievement. However, these quotas will still be significantly higher than the maximum recycling levels set in the packaging directive and concerns over Germany's ability to reprocess so much material remain.

France

In January 1991, the then Minister of the Environment Brice Lalonde asked the chief executive of BSN (one of the world's largest packaging producers) to devise a scheme to collect and recover packaging waste. These proposals lead to the creation of an organisation called *Eco-Emballages*, which was set up to subsidise the collection and sorting of packaging waste.

On 1 April 1992 a 'Décret' on household packaging waste collection and disposal was published. The Décret had a number of key elements:

- the responsibility for waste collection would remain with local authorities (unlike in Germany);
- the packaging industry was to levy itself in order to fund the costs of waste packaging recovery;
- only companies taking back their own packaging would be excluded from the levy;
- companies taking part in the levy scheme would be entitled to use the Green Dot logo (following agreement with DSD);
- incineration with energy recovery was considered a valid form of recovery;
- a target of recovering 75 per cent of all packaging waste by the year 2000 was set;
- a FF20 per tonne landfill levy was to be introduced, to be collected by ADEM, the French Environmental Protection Agency, and used to support recycling infrastructure developments.

Fees charged for the use of the Green Dot vary from 10 centimes for packaging with a volume greater than 30 litres to 0.5 centimes for packaging with a volume of between 50–200 ml. These rates are approximately one-tenth of those charged in Germany.

A target was set of recovering (or 'valorising', to use the French term) 75 per cent of all packaging waste, with no individual material reaching less than 60 per cent valorisation. Recycling is to increase from 0.9m tonnes per annum in 1992 to 1.35m tonnes per annum in 1996 and incineration from 0.4m to 0.7m tonnes over the same period.

The FF20 per tonne landfill levy was expected to raise FF500m each year, which would be used to finance the building of 160 waste treatment plants over a ten year period.

On 29 November 1992 the French Government formally approved the establishment of Eco-Emballages, which came into existence on 1 January 1993. It is 50 per cent owned by ECOPAR, a private company which is in turn owned by one hundred users of packaging, such as Colgate Palmolive, Proctor & Gamble, BSN and L'Oréal, each of whom had a 1 per cent share. Glass packaging is not included within the operations of Eco-Emballages. The wine, beer and spirits producers set up their own scheme called Adelphe, which works in partnership with Eco-Emballages. The operation of Eco-Emballages and Adelphe is illustrated in Figure 11.2.

Companies participating in Eco-Emballages pay a levy, which effectively subsidises the prices paid to local authorities for the collected and sorted materials. For example, local authorities receive FF150 per tonne for collected glass from the glass reprocessing industry, plus FF50 per tonne from Eco-Emballages. For plastics, they receive nothing except the cost of transport from the plastics reprocessors, but

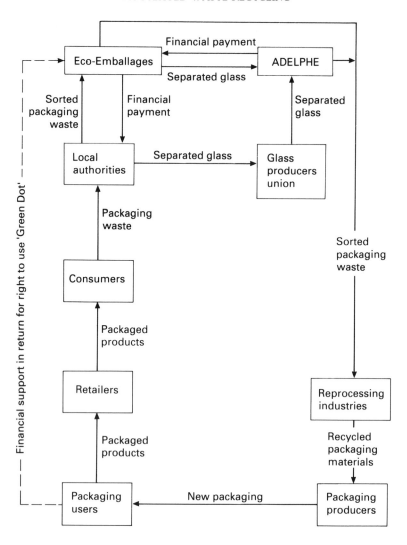

Figure 11.2 The operation of Eco-Emballages

FF1500 from Eco-Emballages. The target for levy collection is FF 700m per annum by 1996, to subsidise 90 local authority contracts, covering 10 million citizens.

The Netherlands

The Netherlands has a particular problem with waste disposal, in that if you dig a hole it tends to fill up with water. Landfill is so expensive that incineration and recycling are more developed in the Netherlands than in many other European countries.

In June 1991 the Dutch Government and industry signed a Packaging Covenant which had two primary objectives:

1)   to reduce the quantities of packaging consumed to 1986 levels by the year 2000 (with a possible further reduction of 10 per cent on these levels);
2)   to increase the rate of recycling of packaging waste to at least 60 per cent by the year 2000 (the recycling rate in 1986 was of the order of 25 per cent).

The Netherlands is so far the only country in Europe which has set a target for the reduction of packaging. The 1986 level of packaging consumption was approximately 2 million tonnes per annum and it is predicted that if no action is taken, this level will increase to 2.8m tonnes per annum by the year 2000. The target that has been set thus represents a 30 per cent reduction against predicted levels of packaging consumption. The reduction is to be achieved by reducing the thickness of packaging materials, avoiding unnecessary packaging and packing less air, that is, ensuring the pack is no bigger than the product being packed.

The covenant also includes a provision to ban the use of certain materials which are considered harmful (such as PVC) and a proposed ban on the landfilling of packaging waste by the year 2000. Incineration is expected to rise to 40 per cent to complement the 60 per cent recycling rate target.

The Dutch packaging manufacturers and users formed an industry organisation called Stichting Verpakking en Milieu (SVM) to fulfil their obligations under the Packaging Covenant. SVM was given the following objectives, to:

- create the necessary recycling facilities and use the recycled materials collected, in order to meet the recycling target;
- ensure that all collected glass is colour separated at source (by 1994);
- offer house to house collection of used dry packaging (paper and cartons) – 50 per cent by 1995 and 75 per cent by the year 2000;
- commence trial projects for separate collection systems in 1991/92 and evaluate the results by 1993 at the latest;
- use identification symbols to assist in the separate collection and sorting of packaging waste; and
- establish with the Dutch government an intensive programme of public education on packaging recycling.

Some immediate objectives were also set:

1)   a ban on gift packaging of spirit bottles;
2)   weight reductions in beverage cartons;
3)   discussions with retailers to reduce promotional packaging;
4)   a ban on free carrier bags;
5)   the encouragement of refill systems for detergents; and
6)   an investigation of substitutes for PVC and blister packs.

143

Longer term specific aims included:

- the promotion of concentrated detergents;
- lightweighting of glass and metal beverage containers;
- a ban on shrink-wrapping of pet food trays; and
- an increase in the size of toothpaste tubes.

The targets set in the Packaging Covenant are clearly ambitious, but the size of the country, the relationship that exists between the government and industry and the understanding amongst consumers of the need for recycling which already exists, suggests that these targets could be obtained.

Belgium

In 1993, the Belgian government passed legislation which would lead to the introduction of so-called 'eco-taxes' from 1 January 1994 (the introduction was subsequently delayed until 1 January 1995). These taxes would be applied to five categories of product as follows:

1) paper and cardboard would incur a tax of BF10 per kilo except for paper used in the printing of books, technical and special papers and paper and board for wrapping food;
2) a tax of BF20 would be applied to batteries unless they were returnable to suppliers with a minimum deposit of BF10;
3) disposable razors and cameras would be taxed at BF10 and BF300 respectively (recyclable cameras would be taxed at only BF10);
4) a tax of BF15 would be levied on bottles and cans of mineral water, beer and soft drinks unless they were reusable with a minimum deposit of BF7 for containers sized 50cl or over and BF3.50 for containers under 50cl;
5) industrial packaging for certain products, such as pesticides, would be subject to an eco-tax, as would the products themselves, on the basis of their toxicity.

Both paper and board and beverage containers would be exempt from the taxes if they met certain recycling criteria:

- Paper and board packaging would be exempt if certain grades met targets for recyclability and for recycled content, for example:
  - newsprint would not be taxed if 55 per cent was recyclable;
  - tissue paper is to contain a minimum of 15 per cent recycled fibre content;
  - woodfree printing and copy paper is to contain a minimum of 80 per cent recycled fibre.

- Bottles and cans for mineral water, beer and soft drinks would be exempt from the taxes provided at least 80 per cent of glass, aluminium and tinplate containers were produced from recycled material and 70 per cent of plastics was collected and recycled at the expense of the suppliers.

144

These proposals have attracted fierce criticism in Belgium, notably from the paper industry and the indigenous Belgian PVC industry (as a result the implementation of the tax on PVC containers was delayed until 1 July 1994). The targets do seem somewhat arbitrary, for example the target for paper tissue containing a 15 per cent recycled fibre content by 1996 is below the *current* European average. The European paper industry federation CEPI has also stated that to achieve a recycled fibre content of 50 per cent for printing and copy paper by 1995 using current technology would increase the costs of such paper significantly.

The objective of the proposed eco-taxes is not, however, to raise money, but rather to stimulate actions such as recycling, so that the taxes are never actually levied. If money *is* raised, it will be passed to the three regional governments in Belgium to finance environmental improvements such as polluted site clean-up, environmental research and pilot projects.

The Belgian packaging industry has responded to the eco-tax proposals by setting up an organisation called FOST PLUS, which it is anticipated will operate along similar lines to the French Eco-Emballages from 1 January 1994.

The UK position on packaging

The UK packaging industry has been extremely concerned about the possibility of an approach to waste packaging similar to that taken in Germany and France being imposed upon them, either directly by the UK government, or indirectly as a result of EU legislation. The approach of the industry has been to attempt to demonstrate that realistic levels of recycling can be achieved at little or no additional cost to existing waste management practices. This response was initially led by an organisation called The Consortium of the Packaging Chain (COPAC). This was an umbrella organisation comprising representatives of the trade associations who act on behalf of both the packaging industry and the secondary raw materials industries. In October 1992 COPAC presented a plan to the government[51] which stated that a target of recycling 43 per cent of packaging as material by the year 2000 was both realistic and achievable and that the packaging industry was prepared to commit itself to this target.

Clearly, we can learn much from what has happened already in other European countries, in particular with regard to the problems in Germany. Four key issues need to be addressed in any plan to develop the recycling of packaging in the UK.

First, any proposed scheme for the handling of packaging waste must provide incentives to reduce the generation of such waste and not focus simply on recycling ever increasing amounts of waste. Of the three countries which have implemented national packaging schemes, only the Netherlands has addressed this issue. Any proposal for the UK must include this requirement and credit its achievement in any targets which are set. One way to achieve this would be to set targets to reduce the proportion of waste being disposed of, rather than targets to increase the proportion being recycled, leaving industry free to select the most appropriate recovery methods.

Secondly, there are strong arguments for the collection of all waste, including packaging for recycling, remaining the responsibility of local authorities. Local authorities have a legal duty to undertake such collections and have developed efficient and cost effective collection techniques. Any system for collecting waste packaging should thus be integrated into existing arrangements in order to minimise cost and maximise efficiency. However, an appropriate mechanism for funding the costs of recycling must be devised to achieve this.

Thirdly, any increase in the amount of material being collected for recycling must be matched by increases in the capacity of the reprocessing industries to process such material. The balance of supply and demand must be managed, something which cannot be achieved through existing pricing mechanisms alone. The consequences of failing to address this issue have been graphically demonstrated in Germany.

Finally, the marginal cost of recycling compared with waste disposal could be significantly reduced when the government introduces the much talked about landfill tax in April 1996. A landfill tax should both encourage waste minimisation and reduce the additional costs of recycling, which the packaging industry is effectively being asked to fund.

The Producer Responsibility initiative

In July 1993, the new Secretary of State for the Environment John Gummer MP and the President of the Board of Trade Michael Heseltine MP, effectively rejected the COPAC proposal and gave the packaging industry until Christmas 1993 to come up with a plan to ensure the recovery of between 50 per cent and 75 per cent of all packaging by the year 2000. If such a plan was not forthcoming the ministers stated their intention to legislate in order to achieve their objectives.

In order to achieve this target, a group of 28 companies, drawn from the packaging industry, were set the following objectives by the ministers:

■ to establish an effective organisation to prepare and implement the plan;
■ to commit the industry to funding the required collection and processing capacity and to establish a mechanism to raise the required funding;
■ to develop a stage plan to reach the 50 per cent to 75 per cent recovery target by the year 2000, but also to expand the existing collection and processing capacity within the next year;
■ for industry to be willing to increase the demand for recycled materials;
■ for immediate action to be taken to safeguard the UK paper and plastics recycling infrastructure which was threatened by subsidised foreign imports.

In response to this challenge, the Producer Responsibility Industry Group (the PRG) as the group of 28 companies become known, published a plan entitled 'Real Value from Packaging Waste' in February 1994[52] (subsequently republished in October 1994). The targets to be achieved by this plan are an overall recovery rate of 32 per cent in 1993 and 58 per cent in 2000, with recycling rates of 30 per cent and 49 per cent respectively. The plan may be summarised as follows:

- a central organisation called VALPAK will be established to implement and operate the plan;
- each recycled material sector will establish a materials organisation which will agree with VALPAK the funding needs of that material sector; VALPAK will also agree the funding requirements of local authorities and waste management companies involved in collection and processing;
- a levy will be applied to all packaged products to fund the recycling of packaging; the method of calculating the levy and at which point in the supply chain it is to be collected have yet to be determined;
- VALPAK will manage the collection and disbursement of all funds;
- VALPAK will coordinate the establishment of additional household waste collection and processing schemes;
- VALPAK will monitor and report progress against the recovery targets.

The PRG also made it clear that without legislation to ensure that the whole of the packaging industry will comply with the levy scheme, such a scheme would fail. The government made a commitment to introducing such legislation in the Queen's Speech of October 1994.

Having completed the task set by John Gummer, the PRG was formally disbanded in December 1994 and an interim organisation, V-WRAG (the VALPAK Working Representative Advisory Group) established to oversee the creation of VALPAK.

Packaging waste is to be recovered from both household and commercial and industrial sources. Only glass, steel cans, aluminium cans and certain plastic bottles are to be collected from household sources, and only paper and board and plastic packaging will be collected from commercial and industrial sources. The planned recycling targets are shown in Table 11.4. This table illustrates that the main collection of packaging for recycling will be from commercial and industrial sources. Even though household packaging accounts for approximately one half of total packaging waste arisings, only 14 per cent of household waste is reported to have been recycled in 1993 and only 34 per cent of such packaging is targeted for recycling in the year 2000. These relatively low levels of household packaging

Table 11.4 Producer Responsibility Industry Group recycling targets

	1993			2000		
	Packaging waste arisings ('000 tonnes)	Packaging waste to be recycled (%)	Recycling target (%)	Packaging waste arisings ('000 tonnes)	Packaging waste to be recycled (%)	Recycling target (%)
Household packaging	3600	7	23	3757	16	33
Commercial and industrial packaging	3692	23	77	4294	33	67
Total packaging	7292	30	100	8051	49	100

recycling result in part from the decision not to collect paper and board packaging from household sources.

The PRG plan is clearly central to the future development of household waste recycling in this country and has the following implications:

- the collection of recyclable materials will continue to be the responsibility of local authorities;
- only a limited range of packaging materials are to be targeted; and
- for the targeted materials and for selected recycling schemes, financial support will be provided.

However as we will see in the next chapter, the impact of the PRG plan will be significant, but because the main focus of the plan is on commercial waste, its contribution to household waste recycling will be limited, as will its contribution to achieving the government's 25 per cent recycling target.

Clearly, in order to achieve its target of recycling 25 per cent of household waste by the year 2000, the government needs the packaging industry to act to increase the levels of packaging recycling. In order to understand the kinds of changes which might take place as a result of this development, we will briefly examine what currently happens to packaging and packaging waste.

The packaging supply chain

The packaging supply chain is the name given to the series of stages and activities which packaging passes through on its journey from product manufacture to delivery to the consumer. This is illustrated in Figure 11.3. Packaging and the product which the packaging is to contain are manufactured separately and only bought together either at the point where the product is manufactured or, for example in the case of liquid beverages, at a dedicated filler. Packaged products are then distributed either directly to retailers or through regional distribution centres. As far as the packaging industry is concerned this is the end of their responsibility, when the packaged product reaches the retailer. However, as Figure 11.3 shows, the packaging supply chain actually extends beyond the retailer, via the consumer and the waste collector, to the point of final disposal. One of the key objectives of any legislation in this area is to force the packaging industry to accept that they have at least partial responsibility for these later stages of the packaging supply chain.

The packaging industry has invested a great deal of time, money and effort in optimising the flow of goods along the packaging supply chain. Modern methods of transport and distribution are sophisticated and tightly controlled. As products (and their associated packaging) move through the supply chain they become increasingly dispersed, so that when the packaging becomes packaging waste, that is, when it reaches the consumer's dustbin, it is as widely distributed as it possibly could be. This represents one of the basic problems to be faced when attempting to recycle packaging, namely, how to collect it. Attempts to collect packaging waste by pushing it back down the packaging supply chain, as typified by the 'take-back'

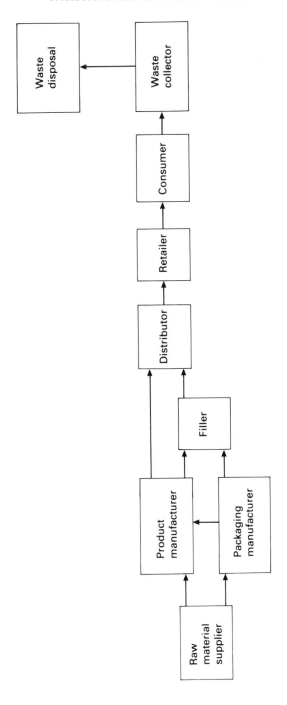

Figure 11.3 The packaging supply chain

obligation included in the German Packaging Ordinance are impractical, because the supply chain has been designed to optimise the flow of goods in one direction only. If the packaging supply chain were to be redesigned in order to facilitate packaging take-back, it is possible that the inefficiencies that this would introduce could lead to a deterioration in the environmental performance of the supply chain, to an extent which might exceed the environmental benefits of recycling. In addition, it is likely that the additional costs associated with such a system would be significant. Packaging take-back is not therefore a viable proposition, but has been used very successfully as a threat to make the packaging industry act, as in the case of Germany.

If we are to achieve the reuse and recycling of packaging, instead of attempting to push things back down the supply chain, we need to create a supply loop. This is illustrated in Figure 11.4, which shows how the different levels of packaging (primary, secondary and tertiary) could be returned for reuse or recycling from different points within the supply chain.

For example, within the existing definition of the supply chain, secondary and tertiary packaging could be returned from retail outlets either to the regional distribution centre or to the filler for reuse. This is already happening for reusable tertiary packaging such as cages or pallets, but could be further developed, particularly for secondary cases or display trays, if these were designed to be reusable rather than disposable. Primary packaging, due to its extreme dispersal, can only be collected either from the household (kerbside collection) or by the householder depositing the material at a collection point (bring system). Following sorting, there is the possibility of some packaging being returned for reuse, for example in the case of wine bottles in France and Germany, however the majority would be reprocessed.

The environmental performance of packaging

When considering any redesign of the packaging supply chain it is important that we consider the environmental impacts of any changes and that we do not fall into the trap of recycling for its own sake. So for example, if a change were proposed for the packaging of liquid beverages, from plastic to glass bottles, because glass was seen to be a more recyclable material, the negative environmental impact of transporting a much heavier material for a given unit of product could in fact outweigh the environmental benefits of recycling. Clearly, any such decision should ideally be based on a full Life Cycle Analysis (LCA), but in the absence of both common agreement on the methods of conducting an LCA and of reliable and available data upon which to base such a decision, we can only rely on common sense to guide us to ensure that such changes do in fact deliver a positive environmental benefit.

Likely developments in packaging

The packaging industry is already beginning to act both to reduce the amount of packaging in use and to identify how waste packaging could be made more

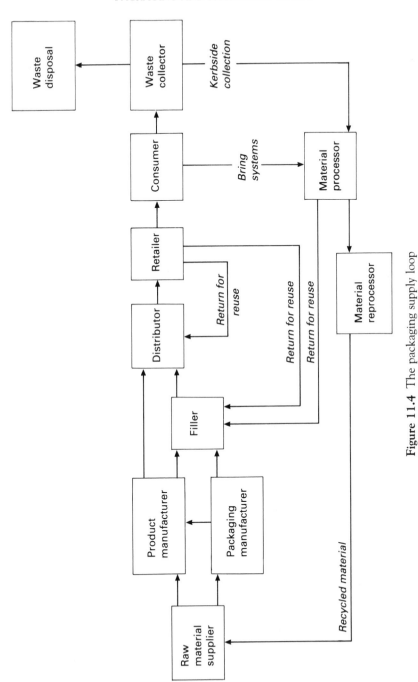

Figure 11.4 The packaging supply loop

recyclable. Such actions are by no means altruistic. The industry is responding to pressure from consumers and is acting in advance of possible legislation. There is also a significant financial incentive for the manufacturing and retail industries to reduce the amount of packaging used, simply to reduce the cost of the product. Clearly packaging manufacturers do not wish to see reductions in the amount of packaging consumed, since like all industries, they would like to see demand for their products increase. Some manufacturers have, however, recognised the possibility of gaining competitive advantage by trading on the environmental performance of their packaging. We are thus witnessing the start of a change in the way our goods are packaged and we can expect to see greater and increasing change if legislation is introduced. These changes are likely to be characterised in the following ways:

- the minimisation of packaging by careful redesign, to ensure that the packaging meets its functional requirements with the minimum material content;
- increasing incidents of reusable packaging particularly at the tertiary and secondary level, with a move to standardisation of such packaging units (for example the reusable plastic box currently being developed for secondary packaging by Schoeller of Germany), to allow such packaging to be returned to any distributor or filler, not necessarily the original user of the packaging;
- moves to make primary and secondary packaging more recyclable, in particular by making materials readily identifiable, by the redesign of packaging to use fewer materials and, where multi-materials are used in one pack, to make these readily separable;
- a possible increase in the recovery as energy of packaging which cannot be recycled as material, due to contamination by food products, the small physical size or its mixed material nature (clearly this would rely on the availability of suitable Waste to Energy plants).

Changes such as those outlined above are already beginning to happen, particularly in continental Europe, in response to national legislation. Some of these changes can also already be seen in this country, as many products are today manufactured for pan-European distribution. For example, the packaging of a product sold in the UK which is also sold in Germany, will have to conform with the German packaging legislation. This is why we are increasingly seeing products in the UK which bear the Green Dot logo.

However, until the PRG plan is adopted, or until the EU packaging directive is finally implemented, the pressure on packaging manufacturers and users to play their part in establishing recycling in this country will be limited. They should however recognise (and many already do) that such change is coming and that it is better to accept this and work with the flow of change rather than to attempt to resist it or to hope that it will not happen. We need industry, central government and local authorities to work together if we are to achieve a sustainable and environmentally beneficial recycling culture in the UK. Each has a significant role to play, but such a grouping is unusual and much work needs to be done to ensure that the necessary mutual understanding, trust and cooperation is developed. We can learn lessons from Germany and take what is best from the Dutch, French and Belgian approaches, but ultimately we must develop a system for packaging waste management which recognises the particular circumstances which prevail in this country.

Given that the focus on packaging will lead to the creation of some form of national scheme for the recycling of these materials, the influence of this issue for the recycling of all materials cannot be understated. The issue of packaging recycling is likely to drive the next phase of the development of recycling in this country, something which should be recognised by all those involved in recycling today. With this in mind, in the next chapter we examine the kinds of developments which are likely and identify the barriers to such developments which remain to be overcome.

CHAPTER TWELVE

THE FUTURE DEVELOPMENT OF RECYCLING IN THE UK

———————— ◆ ————————

Recycling targets

In Chapter 3 we saw that in theory over 50 per cent of household waste is recyclable, and that based on this assumption, the government has set a target of recycling at least one half of this figure, that is 25 per cent of all household waste, by the year 2000. In 1993, we recycled as little as 5 per cent of all household waste, so how is the required five-fold increase in recycling to be achieved?

Taking the data on the composition of household waste from Chapter 3, together with the analysis of the markets in Chapter 8, the two groups of materials which are suitable for recycling are the dry recyclables, representing 63 per cent of household dustbin waste, and the organic garden waste, representing 20 to 60 per cent of household civic amenity site waste. Taking an average of 43 per cent for the organic garden waste, if all of this material were recycled this would represent a recycling diversion rate of 59 per cent of household waste.

Within the dry recyclables, the three categories which are, and which are likely to continue being recycled, are packaging, newspapers (and magazines) and textiles. Taking figures from Table 3.1, these categories represent 23 per cent, 16 per cent and 2 per cent of household dustbin waste respectively. We therefore need to examine how the recycling of these materials and of organic garden waste could develop by the year 2000.

With regard to packaging, the development of recycling will in large part be

Table 12.1 Producer Responsibility Industry Group household waste packaging recycling targets

	1993		2000	
	Million tpa	Household waste (%)[1]	Million tpa	Household waste (%)[1]
Recycled domestic packaging	0.5	2.6	1.3	6.5
Total domestic packaging	3.6	18.0	3.8	18.8

1 Assumes 20m tpa of household waste

determined by the actions of VALPAK, the organisation to be established by the packaging industry. The planned development of household waste packaging recycling, set out in the 'Real Value from Packaging Waste' report[53] is summarised in Table 12.1, in terms of the tonnage targets. Also shown in Table 12.1 are the percentages of total household waste that these tonnages represent.

Table 12.1 indicates that approximately one half of the 5 per cent recycling diversion rate for 1993 was as a result of packaging recycling and that in the year 2000, the contribution from domestic packaging recycling is targeted to rise to 6.5 per cent.

Turning to the other major element of the dry recyclables fraction, newspapers and magazines, taking the collected tonnage figure from Table 8.7 of 542,000 tonnes in 1992, this represents a recycling diversion rate of 2.7 per cent, if all such material came from domestic sources. Given that some of this material will have been collected from non-domestic sources, this figure, together with the 2.6 per cent for packaging, confirms the 5 per cent recycling diversion rate for 1993 (the contribution from organic material composting being negligible in comparison with dry recyclables recycling). Forecasting the level of newsprint recycling in the year 2000 is not easy, however, the newspaper industry has committed itself to seeking to meet a target of all newsprint having a 40 per cent recycled fibre content by the year 2000.

From Table 8.7, the recycled content of UK produced newsprint in 1993 was 28 per cent of consumption, so that a 40 per cent recycled fibre content, assuming no increase in the level of newsprint consumption, would equate to the collection of 773,000 tonnes per annum of waste newspaper, an increase of 232,000 tonnes per annum or 43 per cent compared with 1993. To put this in context, the new SCA paper mill at Aylesford will require approximately 465,000 tonnes per annum of de-inking grades of waste paper for newsprint production. If such an increase in the recycled fibre content of UK produced newsprint were achieved by the year 2000, this would increase the current recycling diversion rate for waste newsprint from 2.7 per cent to 3.9 per cent.

It is very difficult to estimate what could be achieved in terms of textile recycling by the year 2000, but if we are optimistic and apply the government's target of recycling one half of all recyclables to textiles, this would yield a diversion rate of approximately 0.8 per cent.

The future level of organic waste composting is even harder to estimate. Table 3.2 suggests that such waste can constitute between 22 per cent and 64 per cent of household civic amenity site waste. Let us take an average figure of 43 per cent and assume that civic amenity site waste accounts for 20 per cent of all household waste, or 1.7m tpa. If all such organic material were composted this would represent a 8.6 per cent recycling diversion rate. Clearly this level of recycling is unlikely, however, to be consistent with the government's recycling target, let us assume that one half of all such material is composted by the year 2000. This would result in a 4.3 per cent recycling diversion rate from garden waste composting.

If we now add together the likely levels of diversion from packaging, newsprint, textiles and organic garden waste recycling, we can see how likely it is that the government's recycling target will be achieved. This is summarised in Table 12.2, which shows that if the PRG target for household waste packaging is met, if the newsprint industry's target for recycled fibre content is met and if one half of all textiles and civic amenity site garden waste were recycled, the overall national recycling diversion rate would be less than 16 per cent, compared with the Government's target of 25 per cent.

So, what more could be done in order to reach the government's target? It is unlikely that a higher level of textile recycling or organic waste composting would be achieved, indeed it is questionable whether diversion rates as high as 0.8 per cent and 4.3 per cent could be achieved. Any improvement in the diversion rate will, have to come, therefore, from either packaging or newsprint recycling or from another element of household waste.

The PRG targets for household waste packaging recycling quoted in Table 12.1 are based on the scenario presented in their plan, which envisages only 5 per cent of households being serviced by a kerbside collection scheme and 35 per cent and 45 per cent of homes being serviced by high and low density bring schemes respectively. A second scenario is presented in the plan (but not developed into full projections), which assumes 40 per cent of households will be on a kerbside scheme and only 20 per cent and 25 per cent will use high and low density bring facilities.[54] In addition to increases in the anticipated collected tonnages of steel and aluminium cans and plastic bottles, this second scenario also envisages the collection of

Table 12.2 Summary of projected levels of recycling

| | 1993 | | 2000 | |
| | | Recycling | | Recycling |
Waste category	mtpa	diversion rate (%)	mtpa	diversion rate (%)
Packaging	0.5	2.6	1.3	6.5
Newsprint	0.5	2.7[1]	0.8	3.9
Textiles	0.0	0.0	0.2	0.8
Organic garden waste	0.0	0.0	0.9	4.3
TOTAL	1.0	5.3	3.2	15.5

1 Assumes all collected newsprint was from domestic sources

810,000 tpa of newsprint via the kerbside schemes. The effect of this would be to increase the packaging diversion rate in Table 12.2 by 0.7 per cent, to give a total diversion rate of 16.2 per cent (unless there was a further increase in demand for waste newsprint, over and above the 40 per cent target, the collected newsprint would simply displace material collected from other sources). Under this second scenario, recycling diversion rates are claimed to be 48 per cent for steel and aluminium cans and plastic bottles and 58 per cent for glass. It is perhaps surprising that the overall packaging recycling diversion rate is so low, at only 7.2 per cent when the individual material diversion rates are so high. However, it must be remembered that the packaging materials targeted in the plan represent only 16 per cent of the household dustbin waste stream, or 13 per cent of total household waste. This then exemplifies the mismatch which exists between what is planned or deemed practical in terms of which materials can be recycled and the government's recycling target. This situation is summarised in Table 12.3 which shows a theoretical recycling diversion rate for the materials listed of 18 per cent, which is broadly comparable with the 16.2 per cent target calculated above using the PRG scenario 2.

The issue is not, therefore, that the target recycling diversion rates for individual materials are too low, as can be seen if the figure of 15.5 per cent in Table 12.2 is compared with that of 18 per cent in Table 12.3, but rather that the range of materials which it is currently planned or envisaged will be recycled is insufficient to meet the government's target.

The primary categories of recyclable materials which are not included in Table 12.3 and their potential contribution to the overall diversion rate are shown in Table 12.4.

Table 12.3 The materials currently targeted for recycling and their possible contribution to the government's recycling target

Material	Total household waste (%)[1]	Contribution to total recycling diversion rate (%) assuming 50 per cent recycling
Packaging		
■ steel cans	3.4	1.7
■ aluminium cans and foil	0.7	0.4
■ plastic bottles	1.4	0.7
■ glass	7.3	3.7
Packaging sub-total	12.8	6.4
Newsprint	12.8	6.4
Textiles	1.7	0.9
Garden waste[2]	8.6	4.3
TOTAL	35.9	18.0

1 All categories except garden waste based on 80 per cent of figures presented in Table 3.1 (dustbin waste assumed to constitute 16m of the 20m tpa of household waste, that is 80 per cent); 2 Based on 43 per cent of Civic Amenity Site waste

Table 12.4 Recyclable materials currently not targeted for recycling

Material[1]	Total household waste (%)[2]	Contribution to total recycling diversion rate (%) assuming 50 per cent recycling
Other paper	7.6	3.8
Board packaging	3.0	1.5
Other board	2.5	1.3
Paper and board sub-total	*13.1*	6.6
Plastic film	4.2	2.1
Dense plastic (non-bottle)	3.2	1.6
TOTAL	20.6	10.3

1 Category descriptions taken from Table 3.1; 2 Based on 80 per cent of figures presented in Table 3.1 (dustbin waste assumed to constitute 16m of the 20m tpa of household waste, that is 80 per cent)

If a 50 per cent recycling rate could be achieved for all of the materials listed in both Table 12.3 and Table 12.4, an overall diversion rate of 28.3 per cent would be achieved, a figure clearly in line with the government's target. So why are the materials listed in Table 12.4 not being targeted for collection?

While it is true that in some existing schemes some of these materials are being collected, there are no indications that such collection is likely to be encouraged on a national basis. Taking paper and board first, the largest sub-group is that of 'other paper'. Such material comprises a wide range of paper grades and products such as writing paper and envelopes (primarily from official and junk mail), telephone directories, wrapping paper, books, posters and other graphic material. Some of these paper grades are high quality, some are low. The key issue is that given the wide range of paper grades, the relatively low level of arisings and the often small physical size of such material, the necessary separation into single grades of paper is expensive and can only be achieved in a central sorting facility, such as a MRF. With regard to cardboard ('board packaging' and 'other board'), the situation is simpler in that there are effectively only two grades present, KLS and coloured card, but when such material is mixed with the other paper grades, sorting is again expensive.

The situation with regard to non-bottle rigid plastics is similar to that of paper and board in that there are a significant number of different polymers which would require separation, and the plastic items concerned (primarily food packaging such as yoghurt and margarine pots) are often physically quite small. The sorting of such material is thus expensive. Plastic materials also have a very low bulk density so that transporting them any distance for sorting or reprocessing is both expensive and can use more energy than is saved by recycling. It is these two issues which have limited the development of the recycling of post-consumer plastics, particularly in the case of film. As explained in Chapter 7, the reprocessing of plastics, in particular the need for washing is both expensive and energy intensive. An industry report on the potential for the recycling of plastic films[55] suggests that while the recycling of plastic film from commercial and industrial sources saves approximately 34 per cent of the energy used in virgin film production, recycling postconsumer film could use 19 per cent more energy than virgin production. A separate study on the use of recycled film from commercial sources in the production of carrier bags[56] concluded that the energy saving compared with the use of virgin film could be as high as 49 per cent. There thus appears to be evidence in support of the recycling of plastic film, but not from domestic sources. From the point of view of reprocessing, this is in part as a result of the high degree of printing on such film, for example on carrier bags, and the presumed high degree of contamination. This second point is generally only true if the film has been in contact with food or has been contaminated in the collection process.

As a result, the materials listed in Table 12.4 are not currently being targeted for widespread collection because they are considered to be too diverse (in terms of grades or types of material), too contaminated (particularly in the case of plastic film), and too expensive to collect, process and reprocess. By neglecting these materials a possible 10.3 per cent diversion rate will not be achieved. Some of these materials could, however, be successfully recycled if they were included in a commingled kerbside collection and processing scheme. The key to the success of such an approach is the selection of those elements of the materials listed in Table 12.4 which are clean and of a reasonable physical size and which are readily identifiable by the householder to facilitate correct separation at source. Examples of such products include clean plastic carrier and other bags, corrugated cardboard boxes, large rigid plastic food containers such as ice-cream and margarine tubs (HDPE) and cereal packets (coloured card). Such targeting could add of the order of 2–3 per cent to the diversion rate, with little increase in collection costs if these materials were included with an existing or planned commingled material collection service. There would of course be increased processing costs, and these would need to be carefully analysed, particularly in the case of plastic film, using the material cost allocation methods described in Chapter 9.

However, given that a large proportion of the materials listed in Table 12.4 are unsuitable for recycling and indeed also a proportion of those materials listed in Table 12.3, consideration must be given as to the most appropriate method of waste management for dealing with these materials. Clearly, the metals and glass can only be recovered as material, but as we saw in Chapter 4 there are alternative recovery options for the paper, plastics, textiles and organic materials.

For plastics, the only recovery alternative is that of energy recovery by incineration, either in a WTE or CHP plant or as some form of refuse derived fuel. The same options apply to the other materials, but in addition paper, textiles (natural fibres only) and garden waste could be digested to recover energy or recycled as material by composting (provided there is no contamination of the compostible material by hazardous materials). Indeed, an approach to the treatment of all household waste paper, based on composting, was advocated in the WARM system proposal prepared by the Landbank Consultancy for Gateway Foodmarkets.[57] If the level of contamination of such materials were such as to render the compost produced unsuitable for general use, it would still have a low-grade application as stable landfill cover. However, this exemplifies the ongoing debate regarding whether it is better, in terms of environmental benefit, to recover energy from, or to recycle, organic materials.

This debate is far from simple, and all that can be said with any certainty is that the most environmentally beneficial solution will depend on local circumstances and will be based on a combination of treatment options rather than a single solution. The development of the concept of integrated waste management is thus a welcome one, but it is vital both that recycling is treated as a viable method of treatment when developing an integrated waste management strategy, and that we do not take recycling out of context and attempt to recycle for the sake of recycling.

If household waste recycling in this country is to develop from the current low level of activity to anything like the target of 25 per cent, a number of barriers will have to be overcome. These barriers can be summarised as:

- the high cost of recycling relative to disposal;
- the limited markets for recyclable and recycled materials; and
- the attitudes of householders to recycling.

Each of these issues is discussed below.

The cost of recycling

As we have seen in Chapter 9, the cost of recycling is in general higher than the cost of disposal to landfill and of recovering energy via incineration. Because of this there exists a fundamental barrier to the development of recycling since such additional costs would be borne by local authorities and funded by the council tax. Many local authorities are not in a position to contemplate such increases, for example as a result of capping, and the majority are unwilling to expend more than they do currently on recycling.

This fundamental barrier must therefore be, and is beginning to be, addressed in two ways. First, the cost of recycling must be minimised, by the design and development of cost effective and efficient collection and processing schemes, and the integration of such schemes with other forms of waste management. The concept of integrated waste management, outlined in Chapter 4, will have a key role to play in ensuring that not only the costs of recycling, but of all forms of waste management are minimised. In particular with regard to recycling, when preparing their waste management plan, waste regulation authorities must plan seriously for the development of recycling, waste disposal authorities should reflect this plan when letting waste management contracts, and waste collection authorities need to plan for and implement the integration of recyclables and refuse collection. Clearly, the three levels of waste authority need to work closely together to achieve such integration and generally speaking, this is not something which has happened in the past.

There will also have to be a fundamental change in attitude within such waste authorities, away from the current position that disposal is the normal form of waste treatment and that recovery, and recycling in particular, is a minority issue. Only by treating recycling seriously as a viable method of waste management, can the required integration be achieved and the costs reduced. Waste collection authorities will therefore have to develop and implement credible recycling plans (many authorities did not take the requirement to produce such a plan under the EPA seriously or did not see it within the context of integrated waste management), waste disposal authorities will have to develop more flexible waste management contract arrangements and waste regulation authorities must develop integrated waste management plans which provide the framework within which the other authorities can operate.

The second way in which the barrier of cost is beginning to be addressed is by examining methods of funding recycling other than by the council tax. The first example of this is the proposal by the PRG to raise a levy on packaging, which would be used to fund the recycling (and recovery) of packaging waste. The levy would be passed on to the consumer of the packaged products so that the householder would still be paying for recycling, but in this case not through the council tax system. Such a system has much to commend it in that the cost of recycling will be more closely linked to the level of householder waste generation. If such funding is made available it will reduce the problem identified above of local authorities having to fund recycling. At the same time, the risk that such 'external' funding could allow or even encourage inefficient or ineffective recycling schemes to be established or operated must be minimised. One way in which this could be done is by the rigorous use of the costing standard and other performance measures described in Chapters 9 and 10.

Such funding initiatives are therefore to be welcomed, but problems could arise if more than one source of funds were to become available. For example, the PRG are proposing to fund the recycling of packaging. The government has stated that the principle of producer responsibility is to be extended to other products and has already had discussions with the newspaper industry. The situation could become overly complex if, for example, the packaging industry were funding the collection and processing of packaging in a particular recycling scheme and the newspaper industry were funding the collection and processing of newsprint in the same scheme. The problem could be even more complex if the principle of producer responsibility were extended to the material which creates most problems in household waste management, that of organic waste.

This situation could be accommodated if all costs could be accurately allocated to the different materials concerned, but as we have seen in Chapter 9, that is not yet possible. However, the fundamental issue is a simple one: given that it is the consumer who will ultimately pay for the recycling of the different materials, why is it necessary to develop different and complex administration procedures for different categories of materials?

Again we come back to the principle of integration. There is a danger that we could introduce unnecessary complexity if individual elements of the waste stream are singled out for particular attention. We must ensure that whatever action is taken, including funding provision, is carried out in such a way as to maximise simplicity and integration and minimise complexity and cost.

Market barriers

As we have seen in Chapter 8, there are two markets to be considered, the market for recyclable materials and that for recycled materials. These two markets are inextricably linked.

The lack of available end markets is the reason most often quoted for the current low level of recycling and is frequently cited as a major barrier to future development. For example, in the Coopers & Lybrand survey of waste recycling plans,[58] 64 per cent of local authorities identified the lack of market availability as a barrier to action, with the lack of funding being the second most significant barrier (cited by 57 per cent of authorities). These two issued are directly linked, since the income from the sale of the recyclable materials is often expected to fund collection and processing activities, and when the markets do not offer prices which are sufficiently high to do so, this can be interpreted as a lack of market availability.

In order to understand the real market barriers, we need to separate the issue of funding (and prices offered by the markets) from that of the capacity of the markets to reprocess recyclable material. If the capacity is available but not being used to reprocess recyclable material because it is not financially attractive to the markets to do so, this could be corrected by, for example, the producer responsibility funding mechanisms outlined above. However, if the reprocessing capacity simply does not exist then we have to address a more fundamental problem.

Chapter 8 demonstrated that there is a strong and potentially unlimited demand for steel and aluminium cans, and for textiles and for glass with the exception of green glass. Green glass and paper and board are the two material categories for which any significant increase in the levels of collection could exceed the available capacity to reprocess these materials. In both cases, the current recycling rate is approaching the reprocessing limits of existing UK production capacity, however, in both cases the recycling rate in terms of UK consumption is relatively low (42 per cent for green glass and 62 per cent for paper and board) due to the high level of imports. This presents us with both a problem and an opportunity. If we are to increase the level of recycling of these materials we need to develop new reprocessing capacity, and if this additional capacity is used to produce products which are identical to those which are currently consumed, then there is an opportunity to reduce imports. However, the opportunities for import substitution may be limited, for example because recyclable material such as packaging is not the prime import, rather it is the product within the packaging that is imported and unless that product could in future be packaged in the UK, the opportunities for import substitution are limited. We are therefore faced with the problem that in such cases there is a limit to the quantity of the recyclable material which can be reprocessed into its original form, since there is a limit to the demand for the recycled materials.

In such cases, where consumption exceeds domestic production, alternative uses for the excess recyclable material will have to be found if recycling is to develop. Examples of such diversification include the production from waste paper and board of animal bedding and moulded board products for use in car interiors. Similarly imaginative alternative uses will have to be found for green glass if it cannot be recycled back into packaging.

As has been discussed in Chapter 8, one of the aspects of the markets for recycled materials which needs to be addressed is that of product specifications which currently either preclude or discourage the use of recycled material. This situation needs to be addressed so that the product specification is based on performance rather than the origin of the material. This will increasingly become an issue as we seek to find alternative uses for recycled materials and introduce them into areas where previously only virgin materials have been used.

The other major factor currently limiting the demand for recycled materials is that of consumer acceptance of products with a recycled content, or rather a general prejudice against them. This remains a significant barrier and the approach to changing this attitude is discussed below.

Householder attitudes

The attitude of householders is fundamental to the success or otherwise of two key aspects of recycling: the collection of recyclable materials and the market demand for recycled materials.

Any recycling scheme, whether based on bring or kerbside collection, relies on the voluntary actions of householders to correctly separate the targeted materials at source. If the householder gets this separation wrong, the subsequent processing may not be possible or will be more expensive. Some people will go to great lengths to sort and separate their wastes but they are in the minority, so if recycling is to be developed on a large scale, the methods of separation and storage of recyclable materials must be simple and easy for householders to use.

Many people already use drop-off sites and more would do so if the number of sites were increased. However, given the physical effort involved in taking recyclables to such sites, the number of people prepared to do this must be limited. In addition, since the materials must be stored somewhere until a sufficient quantity has accumulated to justify such a trip, the range of materials that people can be expected to store and then transport to a drop-off site must also be limited.

Given the relative ease of use of kerbside schemes, it is likely that the major growth in collection will come from such methods. However, in order to ensure acceptance and correct and continued use, such systems must be kept simple. For example, most householders can cope with two different collection containers, but it is unlikely that many would accept more than three. So two wheeled bins, one of which may or may not be divided, two Blue Box containers and a refuse container or two different coloured bags would appear to be the practical limit of the degree of separation acceptable to householders (assuming that the property can accept more than one container). Equally, the range of materials that householders are asked to identify and separate must be limited if such separation is to succeed. It is thus far simpler for householders to put all paper and board and all plastic items into a recyclables collection container than it is for them to identify and separate only certain grades or polymers. However, the ease of householder use must be balanced against the subsequent cost of processing.

Whatever methods of collection are employed, it is vital that adequate explanation and education is provided to householders when these new methods are introduced. Not only is this necessary to ensure the correct use of the collection containers, but also to motivate the householders to make the effort required and to explain why it is important and what benefits will result from householders becoming involved. Given that for most schemes to date participation has been voluntary, such education and promotion is vital to convince people to join in; recycling schemes have to be sold to householders. One of the most successful ways of achieving this education is via children. Many schools now teach children about recycling and when a new collection scheme is introduced, it is often the children who are best at identifying which items go in which collection container, and can explain to their parents what happens to the recyclable material and why recycling is important. When planning the introduction of any new recycling scheme, it is thus important to provide information to the schools in the area and to involve them as much as possible.

It is equally important to provide feedback to residents on the success of a recycling scheme. It is to be hoped that separation at source will become a habit over time, rather than being a conscious effort, but until that happens, regular feedback can do much to maintain the commitment of participating householders.

The second aspect of householder attitudes which it is vital to develop if recycling is to expand, is that of their perception of products produced from recycled materials. As we saw in Chapter 8, there is a degree of consumer prejudice against recycled products and unless this prejudice is overcome through education, the markets for recyclable materials will be limited. Consumers must be encouraged not only to buy recycled products, but actively to seek out and demand such products if the recycling loop is to be closed. This message needs to be included in the promotion of any recycling scheme and as much information as possible provided on the availability of existing products, their performance and the benefits which derive from purchasing them in preference to the virgin equivalent. If householders are to be encouraged to separate their recyclable materials at source, they need to see the results of their efforts all around them, whether it is recycled writing paper in stationary shops, recycled plastic street furniture or household products sold in recycled plastic bottles. The proposed symbol contained in the EU Directive on Packaging and Packaging Waste addresses this need and would show the recycled content of any packaging. Thus metal cans and glass containers, which contain a proportion of recycled material would be readily identifiable and would make a major contribution to the feedback required to maintain the householders' commitment to recycling. The use of such a symbol should be extended to cover all products, not just packaging. If we cannot see the fruits of our labours, will we continue to labour?

The way forward

The level of household waste recycling in this country is currently very low and there is a general acceptance that it should be significantly increased. Despite the government's recycling target, the present proposals for the development of recycling are unlikely to achieve more than 17 per cent. With some further expansion, however, 20 per cent could be possible.

Targets have a useful role to play in stimulating change, but they should not be taken as absolutes. For example, the government's target is based on a national average, so that some areas will be expected to recycle more than 25 per cent and some less. However, the majority of local authorities who have set a target have adopted the 25 per cent figure irrespective of whether it is appropriate to their local circumstances.

This issue of appropriateness to local circumstances is a key one. Recycling makes sense if recyclable material can be collected and processed close to the reprocessing markets. If however, such collection is remote from the markets and there is a local WTE plant available is it better to recycle or recover energy? As we have seen in Chapter 4, recycling and energy recovery can be compatible rather than conflicting methods of waste management, provided such coordination is planned for. Such planning is in part the responsibility of the waste regulation authorities when preparing their waste management plans, and in part that of the waste disposal authorities when developing their waste management strategy and letting contracts. But there is also a requirement for planning at a regional and a national level. At the regional level, consideration must be given to the location and size of key facilities such as MRFs or WTE plants to ensure that economies of scale are realised and transport impacts minimised. At a national level, initiatives are required to ensure that the location of new reprocessing capacity is matched to those areas where it is most beneficial for recycling to be developed. Such national planning should be undertaken by the industries concerned but both the PRG and the government could have a role to play.

There is much work to be done if recycling is to be developed to a stage where it has become as routine an activity as landfill is now, but this work has to be undertaken if we are to realise the contribution that appropriate recycling can undoubtedly make to improving and sustaining our environment. Recycling is not as simple a subject as many people might believe, and when it is taken as only one element of an integrated approach to waste management, this complexity is greatly increased in terms of the issues involved, the techniques to be selected and the financial and environmental evaluation which is necessary to ensure that real benefits are achieved. We are undoubtedly making progress, but the recycling of household waste in this country is in its infancy. If recycling is to develop, those responsible for waste management, both national and local government and private companies in the waste management industry, must take recycling seriously as a waste treatment option and understand the benefits and limitations of recycling. Ultimately, however, the responsibility for the development of recycling rests with the individual, with all of us. A local authority can set up a recycling collection scheme, but if we do not use it and use it correctly, recycling will fail. If recyclable material is collected, processed and reprocessed, but we do not buy the products containing the recycled material, recycling will fail. If we do not understand and accept that the present methods of waste disposal are unsustainable and accept that we will have to pay more if we want our waste to be treated in a sustainable manner, recycling will fail. It is up to each and every one of us to play our part in the development of recycling.

REFERENCES

———————◆———————

1 'MSI Data Report : Waste Management : UK', Table 2, p 4, Marketing Strategies for Industry Ltd, July 1992

2 'Assessment of Waste Disposal Data and the Waste Management Market', Table 2.2, p 5, Gibb Environmental Sciences, April 1992

3 'Digest of Environmental Protection and Water Statistics', Table 7.1, p 77, HMSO 1992

4 'COPAC Action Plan to Address UK Integrated Solid Waste Management', Annex 4, p 3, COPAC October 1992

5 'This Common Inheritance – Britain's Environmental Strategy', p 190, HMSO September 1990

6 'Waste: Somebody Else's Problem? Our Choices and Responsibilities', pp 8–9, Biffa Waste Services Ltd, 1993

7 Economic instruments and Recovery of Resources from Waste, HMSO 1992

8 'A Waste Strategy for England and Wales' Consultative Draft, Department of the Environment and the Welsh Office, January 1995

9 The European Recovery and Recycling Association 'Reference Codification Programme – Programme Ratios', January 1994

10 House of Lords Select Committee on the European Communities 26th Report 'Packaging and Packaging Waste', p 18, HL Paper 118, HMSO October 1993

11 House of Commons Environment Select Committee Second Report on Recycling Volume 1, p xxi, 63–1, HMSO, June 1994

12 Sustainable Development – The UK Strategy, Cm 2426, HMSO, January 1994

13 Economic Instruments and Recovery of Resources from Waste, HMSO 1992

14 Waste Management Paper No 28 – Recycling, HMSO 1991

15 A Survey of English Local Authority Recycling Plans, HMSO 1993

16 Atkinson, W, New, R 'Kerbside Collection of Recyclables from Household Waste in the UK – A Position Study', Warren Spring Laboratory report LR946, p 6, May 1993

17 Waste Management Paper No 28, Table 4.2, p 27, HMSO 1991

18 The Technical Aspects of Controlled Waste Management, National Household Waste Analysis Programme, Phase 2 Volume 1 Report on Composition and Weight Data

CWM 082/94, Department of the Environment Wastes Technical Division, August 1994

19 The Technical Aspects of Controlled Waste Management, Development of the National Household Waste Analysis Programme, Summary Report CWM/059/93, Annex 2, Department of the Environment Wastes Technical Division January 1993

20 Waste Management Paper No 28, Table 4.1, p 26, HMSO 1991

21 'A Survey of Local Authority Recycling Plans', Figure 3.3

22 ibid Figure 3.4

23 Royal Commission on Environmental Pollution, Seventeenth Report – Incineration of Waste, Cm 2181, Table 3.4, p 20, HMSO 1993

24 ibid p 37

25 ibid p 56

26 ibid p 70

27 ibid p 91

28 ibid p 85

29 USA Environmental Protection Agency, Dioxin Reassessment Report, November 1994

30 Royal Commission on Environmental Pollution. Seventeenth Report – Incineration of Waste CM 2181 pp 44–47, HMSO, 1993

31 ibid p 62

32 Poll, J 'Kerbside Collection Schemes in the UK', p 5, Paper No W91178(MR) MER4 Conference Belgium, Warren Spring Laboratory, March 1992

33 Wheatley, R J 'Waste-to-Energy – An Overview of Incineration', p 8, Association Energy Projects plc, February 1993

34 Strange, K 'Materials Recycling and Energy Recovery – Partners not Competitors', p 149, Proc Recycling Council Annual Seminar 'Why Recycle', Balkema 1994

35 Waste Management Paper No 28, Table 4.1, p 26, HMSO 1991

36 Detinning Process of Post Consumer Cans – P A Neenan, Rec '93 Conference Proceedings, Geneva, pp 264–268, Hexagon Ltd 1993

37 Bardos, R P 'Survey of Composting in the UK and Europe', Demos seminar, 9 September 1992, Glasgow

38 Atkinson, W, New, R 'Kerbside Collection of Recyclables from Household Waste in the UK – A Position Study', Warren Spring Laboratory report LR946, p 6, May 1993

39 PIFA, OPMA and FPA 'Management of Waste Plastic Packaging Films', Table 1, p 4, June 1991

40 Coopers & Lybrand 'The Cost of Recycling – A Standardised Approach', February 1994

41 National Solid Wastes Management Association 'Specialist Report – The Cost to Recycle at a Materials Recovery Facility', Washington USA

42 Department of the Environment Wastes Technical Division 'Household Waste Recycling Performance Indicators', Technical Review 023, September 1993

43 Waste Management Paper No 28, p 26, Table 4.1

44 European Recovery and Recycling Association 'Reference Codification Programme – Programme Ratios', November 1992

45 'Monitoring and Evaluating Household Waste Recycling Programmes : Waste Definition and Monitoring Parameters', DoE Report CWM/070/93, p 25, Civic Amenity Waste Disposal Project, Luton College of Higher Education, March 1993

46 Department of the Environment Wastes Technical Division 'Household Waste Recycling Performance Indicators', Technical Review 023, September 1993

47 'Monitoring and Evaluating Household Waste Recycling Programmes: Waste Definition and Monitoring Parameters', DoE Report CWM/070/93, p 27, Civic Amenity Waste Disposal Project, Luton College of Higher Education, March 1993

48 The Technical Aspects of Controlled Waste Management, Development of the National Household Waste Analysis Programme, Summary Report CWM/059/93, Annex 2, Department of the Environment Wastes Technical Division January 1993

49 European Recovery and Recycling Association 'Reference Codification Programme – Waste Analysis Procedure', March 1993

50 Atkinson, W, New, R 'Kerbside Collection of Recyclables from Household Waste in the UK – A Position Study', Warren Spring Laboratory report LR946, p 6, May 1993

51 The Consortium of the Packaging Chain (COPAC) 'COPAC Action Plan to Address UK Integrated Solid Waste Management', October 1992

52 The Producer Responsibility Group 'Real Value from Packaging Waste – a Way Forward', February 1994

53 The Producer Responsibility Industry Group 'Real Value from Packaging Waste – a Way Forward', Table 1, p 18, February 1994

54 The Producer Responsibility Industry Group 'Real Value from Packaging Waste – a Way Forward', pp 16–17, February 1994

55 PIFA, OPMA and FPA 'Management of Waste Plastic Packaging Films', June 1991

56 Alida Recycling Ltd 'An Analysis of the Recycling of LDPE at Alida Recycling Ltd, Prepared by Nottingham University Consultants Ltd', August 1992

57 Gateway Foodmarkets 'The WARM System – A Proposal for a Model Waste Recovery and Recycling System for Britain', Gateway Foodmarkets Ltd, January 1992

58 Coopers & Lybrand 'A Survey of Waste Recycling Plans', p 19, HMSO 1993

INDEX

◆